SPANISH PICTURE DICTIONARY COLORING BOOK

Over 1500 Spanish Words and Phrases for Creative & Visual Learners of All Ages

Color and Learn

ISBN: 978-1-951949-43-3

Free Book Reveals The 6 Step Blueprint That Took Students **From Language Learners To Fluent In 3 Months**

- **6 Unbelievable Hacks** that will accelerate your learning curve

- **Mind Training:** why memorizing vocabulary is easy

- **One Hack To Rule Them All:** This <u>secret nugget</u> will blow you away...

Head over to **<u>LingoMastery.com/hacks</u>** and claim your free book now!

CONTENTS

INTRODUCTION

The Spanish Picture Dictionary Coloring Book is a fun vocabulary-building tool with illustrations that you can color while studying. It covers an immense range of topics that will help you learn everything related to the Spanish language in daily subjects, from animals and the weather to parts of the house and describing things.

This introduction is a massive guide to help you get started in Spanish and polish your basic grammar, spelling, punctuation and vocabulary skills. Good luck – and **enjoy yourself at all times!**

BASICS OF THE SPANISH LANGUAGE

I. Spelling and pronunciation

a. The Spanish Alphabet – a Built-in Guide to Pronunciation.

Spanish is a phonetic language, meaning that (with very few exceptions) every letter is pronounced a certain way based on the rules. This is good news for the learner, as with a little practice of the pronunciations given in the dictionary and the information presented here, figuring out the pronunciation of new words will be much easier.

The tables below provide information on the alphabet, the names and pronunciations of the individual letters, and a guide to the sounds they produce in words. Note that some sounds are different than those we know in English, especially *jota* and *erre*, so take your time and enunciate.

Letter	Letter name / Pronunciation		Pronunciation guide
a	*a*	*ah*	Like **a** in **father**
b	*be / be grande*	*beh*	Like the English **b** at the beginning of words, pronounced very softly in the middle of words
c	*ce*	*seh*	Like **c** in **cat** before a, o, u; like **c** in **cent** before e, i
d	*de*	*deh*	Like **d** in **door** but with your tongue behind your teeth, almost like **th** in **the**
e	*e*	*eh*	Like **e** in **get**
f	*efe*	*EH-feh*	Same as in English
g	*ge*	*heh*	Like **g** in **get** Before a, o, u; a raspy English **h**, like the **ch** in **Bach** or **Loch** before e, i,

h	*hache*	*AH-cheh*	Always silent, except in **ch** combination (see below)
i	*i / i latina*	*ee / ee lah-TEE-nah*	Like **ee** in feet
j	*jota*	*HOH-tah*	Like a raspy English **h**, like the **ch** in **Bach** or **Loch**
k	*ka*	*kah*	Same as in English
l	*ele*	*EH-leh*	Same as in English
m	*eme*	*EH-meh*	Same as in English
n	*ene*	*EH-neh*	Same as in English
ñ	*eñe*	*EH-nyeh*	Like the **ny** combination in **canyon** (or the **ñ** in the Spanish loanword **jalapeño**)
o	*o*	*oh*	Like the **o** sound in **oak**
p	*pe*	*peh*	As in English
q	*cu*	*koo*	Like English **k** (always used in combination with u)
r	*erre*	*EH-reh*	Like English **r** but softer, almost sounds like a **d**, trilled when it's the first letter
s	*ese*	*EH-seh*	Same as in English
t	*te*	*teh*	Like **t** in **hat** but with your tongue behind your teeth
u	*u*	*oo*	like the **oo** in **school**
v	*uve / ve chica*	*OO-veh / veh CHEE-kah*	Same as in English
w	*uve doble / doble u*	*OO-veh DOH-bleh / DOH-bleh oo*	Same as in English

x	*equis*	*EH-kees*	Same as in English
y	*ye / i griega*	*yeh /* *ee GRYEH-gah*	Same as in English; functions as consonant and vowel
z	*zeta*	*SEH-tah*	Like **s** in English

The following letter combinations are no longer considered separate alphabet characters, but it is vital to understand that they function together as separate sounds.

Letter	Letter name / Pronunciation		Pronunciation guide
che	*che*	*cheh*	Like **ch** in **chat**
ll	*elle*	EH-yeh	Like **y** in **yellow**, **j** in **jaw**, or **sh** in **ship**, depending on the region
rr	*doble erre*	EH-rreh	Strongly trilled

b. Diphthongs

A diphthong is a sound formed by combining two vowels into a single vowel sound, which is pronounced as a single syllable.

Below are examples of Spanish diphthongs and their pronunciations.

DIPHTHONG	PRONUNCIATION	EXAMPLES	PRONUNCIATION
au	*Ow*	auto	*OW*-toh
ai, ay	*Ay*	aire	*AY*-reh
eu	*ehoo**	Europa	*ehoo*-ROH-pah
ei, ey	*Ey*	Seis, rey	*seys, rrey*
ia	*Yah*	media	MEH-*dyah*
ie	*Yeh*	tiempo	TYEHM-*poh*
io	*Yoh*	junio	HOON-*yoh*
iu	*Yoo*	ciudad	*syoo*-DAHD

oi, oy	*Oy*	tiroides, voy	tee-*ROY*-dehs, *voy*
ua	*Wah*	actual	ahk-*TWAHL*
ue	*Weh*	abuelo	ah-*BWEH*-loh
ui	*Wee*	pingüino	peen-*WEE*-noh
uo	*Woh*	cuota	*KWO*-tah

*Note: This diphthong has no equivalent in English. It is a combination of the **eh** and **oo** sounds pronounced together as quickly as possible.*

c. Pronunciation and syllable stress

Just as Spanish is strict about letter pronunciation, the way a word is written tells us where to put the stress. Now that we know how to pronounce the letters; let's move to the rules governing stress on syllables.

All unaccented Spanish words have the stress on the last syllable, unless the word ends in a vowel, an -s, or an -n (which happen to be our present tense verb endings, as we will see later). If the stress falls on any other syllable, it must be marked with an accent. There are four kinds of written accents.

1. *Agudas*

   The last syllable is stressed. A written accent is required if the word ends in a vowel, an -s, or an -n.

   - *Bebé* (baby)
   - *Cantar* (to sing)

2. *Graves*

   The second to last syllable is stressed.

   - *Bebe* (he drinks)
   - *Canto* (I sing)

3. *Esdrújulas*

   The third to the last syllable is stressed.

   - *Sábado* (Saturday)
   - *Matemáticas* (math)

4. *Sobresdrújulas*

   These have the accent before the third to last syllable. These are not very common and are often adverbs or progressive or imperative forms with personal pronouns attached.

   - *Préstamelo* (lend it to me)
   - *Copiándomelo* (making me a copy)

II. Verbs

a. Verb conjugation

Unlike in English, all Spanish verbs are clearly conjugated for mood, tense, person, and number. This is done by adding endings to what we call the verb stem. All verbs have one of the following endings: *ar*, *er*, and *ir*.

Hablar
Comer
Vivir

To conjugate these verbs in the present tense, for example, the ending is removed, and the appropriate ending is added.

	hablar	**com**er	**viv**ir
yo (I)	-o	-o	-o
tú (you, singular informal)	-as	-es	-es
él / ella / usted (he / she / you, singular formal)	-a	-e	-e
nosotros (we)	-amos	-emos	-imos
vosotros / vosotras (you, plural informal)*	-áis	-éis	-ís
ellos / ellas / ustedes (they / they / you, plural formal)	-an	-en	-en

*Note that the *vosotros/as* form is not used in Latin America. Use *ustedes* for plural you, regardless of level of formality.

Like English, Spanish has regular and irregular verbs. Unlike English, there are some common patterns that can help us group irregularities when studying.

A common irregularity is a stem change. This means that in addition to using the verb without its ar / er / ir ending, we make a small change before conjugating.

For example: cerrar→ cerr-→ cierr
perder→ perd→ pierd
sentir→ sent→ sient

We then add the proper ending to the verb stem according to person and number, with the exception of the *nosotros* form, which takes the unaltered verb stem. It is recommended that you learn the present tense stem along with the infinitive when studying.

	cierr-	pierd-	sient-
yo (I)	cierro	pierdo	siento
tú (you, singular informal)	cierras	pierdes	sientes
él / ella / usted (he / she / you, singular formal)	cierra	pierde	siente
nosotros (we)	cerramos	perdemos	sentimos
ellos / ellas / ustedes (they / they / you, plural)	cierran	pierden	sienten

Note that the verbs *ser* (be) and *ir* (go) have highly unusual conjugations in the present tense, which do not follow any pattern.

	ser	ir
yo (I)	soy	voy
tú (you, singular informal)	eres	vas
él / ella / usted (he / she / you, singular formal)	es	va
nosotros (we)	somos	vamos
ellos / ellas / ustedes (they / they / you, plural formal)	son	van

b. Negation

Negative sentences are formed in Spanish by simply placing the word *no* in front of the verb.

Yo (no) tengo camisas.
I (don't) have shirts.

Hoy (no) puedo ir al trabajo.
I can (not) go to work today.

Yo I
Tù You
~~èl/ella/~~
èl he / ella she / usted you
nosotros we
ellos they / ellas they / ustedes you

c. To be or to be.

There are two verbs in Spanish for be, *ser* and *estar*, conjugated in the present tense as follows:

	ser	estar
yo (I)	soy	estoy
tú (you, singular informal)	eres	estás
él / ella / usted (he / she / you, singular formal)	es	está
nosotros (we)*	somos	estamos
ellos / ellas / ustedes (they / they / you, plural formal)	son	están

Ser is generally used to describe something either permanent or long-lasting. It is concerned with *what* or *who*.

Descriptions

(Yo)* soy Alberto. Soy bajo, de piel oscura y gordo. Soy católico.
I am Alberto. I am short, dark-skinned, and fat. I am Catholic.

Ella es joven.
She is young.

*Since all verbs are conjugated according to the person, the subject is unnecessary and usually omitted unless clarification is required.

Occupations

Ellos son doctores.
They are doctors.

Él es enfermero.
He is a nurse.

Characteristics

Ella es hermosa.
She is beautiful.

Time

Es la una y media de la mañana.
It's half past one in the morning.

Origin

Soy de El Salto, Jalisco.
I am from El Salto, Jalisco.

Relationships

Alfredo es mi tío político.
Alfredo is my uncle-in-law.

Estar is generally used to describe position, location, progressive actions, conditions, and emotions. It is concerned with *how*.

Position

Estoy acostado.
I am lying down.

Ustedes están en el trabajo.
You (plural) are at work.

Progressive actions

Estamos comiendo.
We are eating.

Conditions

Estoy muy cansado hoy.
I am very tired today.

Emotions

Ella está triste hoy.
She is sad today.

In certain expressions, the use of *ser* or *estar* can change the meaning. Some examples are provided below.

SER EXPRESSION	ENGLISH MEANING	*ESTAR* EXPRESSION	ENGLISH MEANING
ser aburrido	to be boring	estar aburrido	to be bored
ser borracho	to be a drunk	estar borracho	to be drunk
ser listo	to be clever	estar listo	to be ready
ser malo	to be bad	estar malo	to be ill
ser seguro	to be safe	estar seguro	to be certain
ser vivo	to be sharp	estar* vivo	to be alive

*Life (unlike death) falls under a temporary state, but *estar* is used with these two descriptions.

d. Word Order

Word order in Spanish is generally subject + verb + object, although some leeway is allowed, and native speakers might not follow this pattern as frequently.

Yo tengo una camisa.
I have a shirt.

Ellos manejan un auto negro.
They drive a black car.

Even questions follow this pattern, with context given by punctuation when writing and intonation when speaking.

¿Ellos manejan un auto negro?
Do they drive a black car?

III.   Nouns

In Spanish, all nouns have grammatical gender. This means that all persons, places, things, and ideas are either masculine or feminine in Spanish.

Unfortunately, there is no real rhyme or reason to these genders, so it is recommended that you always learn the article with the noun.

Examples:

El zapato (the shoe) is masculine.
La camisa (the shirt) is feminine.

Most masculine words end with an -o, while feminine words almost always end with an -a. This is not true in all cases, but it is a reasonable guideline for beginners.

Remember that nouns must always agree with the article in gender and number, so *el zapato / la camisa* (the shoe / the shirt), and *los zapatos / las camisas* (the shoes / the shirts).

IV. Adjectives

In Spanish, adjectives must always agree with the noun they modify in gender and number. For example:

	Singular	Plural
Masculine	*El zapato negro* (the black shoe)	*Los zapatos negros* (the black shoes)
Feminine	*La casa negra* (the black house)	*Las casas negras* (the black houses)

Also, adjectives are generally placed after the noun, with very few exceptions, so *las negras casas* would sound as wrong to a Spanish speaker as *the houses black* would sound to English speakers.

V. Vocabulary

While English is considered a Germanic language, over half of the vocabulary is taken from Latin, the source for Spanish, so a great number of words are very similar in Spanish and English. Below are some common patterns to keep in mind while building your vocabulary.

- -ty→-dad
    - ability / habilidad
    - city / ciudad
    - liberty / libertad
    - quality / calidad

- -ate→-ar
    - accumulate / acumular
    - eliminate / eliminar
    - penetrate / penetrar
    - initiate / iniciar

- -tion→-ción
    - civilization / civilización
    - collection / colección
    - emotion / emoción
    - selection / selección

- -sion→sión
    - dimension / dimensión
    - supervision / supervisión
    - illusion / ilusión
    - profession / profesión

- -ic→-ico/-ica (depending on the gender)
    - cynic / cínico/cínica
    - linguistic / lingüístico/lingüística
    - euphoric / eufórico/eufórica
    - allergic / alérgico/alérgica

- -ous→-oso/-osa (depending on the gender)
    - famous / famoso/famosa
    - curious / curioso/curiosa
    - fabulous / fabuloso/fabulosa
    - disastrous / desastroso/desastrosa

- -ance / ancy→-ancia
    - ambulance / ambulancia
    - substance / sustancia
    - vagrancy / vagancia
    - instance / instancia

- -tor→-dor/-dora (depending on the gender)
    - administrator / administrador/administradora
    - senator / senador/senadora
    - narrator / narrador/narradora
    - facilitator / facilitador/facilitadora

- -ist→-ista
    - artist / artista
    - tourist / turista
    - realist / realista
    - pianist / pianista

- -al→-al
    - casual / casual
    - digital / digital
    - animal / animal
    - confessional / confesional

- -ct→-cto
    - act / acto
    - dialect / dialecto
    - insect / insecto
    - perfect / perfecto/perfecta

- -ar→-ar
    - regular / regular
    - solar / solar
    - lunar / lunar
    - circular / circular

- -ary→-ario
  - glossary / glosario
  - primary / primario/primaria
  - necessary / necesario/necesaria
  - concessionary / concesionario/concesionaria

- -ant→-ante
  - important / importante
  - elegant / elegante
  - distant / distante
  - errant / errante

- -able / -ible→-able / -ible
  - possible / posible
  - responsible / responsable
  - movable / movible
  - accessible / accesible

- -ment→-mento
  - department / departamento
  - document / documento
  - cement / cemento
  - fragment / fragmento

Remember that this is only a guide and that all rules have exceptions. (For example, *locación* is not common in Spanish, and *ubication* is archaic in English; however, the word for location in Spanish is *ubicación*).

Now let's get into the fun stuff and start coloring!

Some pages have been designed for you to flip the book horizontally to get a more beautiful illustration.

Finally, we've added a few quizzes throughout the book for you to test your knowledge. You can find the answers to the quiz at the end of the book.

Added Bonus: 5-Day Spanish Masterclass

This book will no doubt help grow your Spanish vocabulary.

But did you know there are "methods" that can help you learn Spanish up to 325% faster?

This "method" is absolutely something you must add to your arsenal and that's why we have created a **5-Day Spanish Masterclass** for you to take part in.

You'll learn:

- A proven method to help you learn up to 325% faster (according to researchers)
- How to understand Spanish speakers when they talk too fast
- Important vocabulary that could save your life (yes, save your life!)

And much more.

As you've bought this book, you've been granted free access to this masterclass.

Join the 5-Day Spanish Masterclass at <u>LingoMastery.com/SpanishMasterclass</u>

EMOCIONES (EMOTIONS)

1) **feliz** (happy)
feh-LEES

2) **triste** (sad)
TREES-teh

3) **emocionado** (excited)
eh-moh-syoh-NAH-doh

4) **molesto/enojado** (angry)
moh-LEHS-toh/eh-noh-HAH-doh

5) **sorprendido** (surprised)
sohr-prehn-DEE-doh

6) **preocupado** (concerned)
preh-oh-koo-PAH-doh

7) **asustado** (scared)
ah-soos-TAH-doh

8) **curioso** (curious)
koo-RYOH-soh

9) **entretenido/divertido** (amused)
ehn-treh-teh-NEE-doh/dee-vehr-TEE-doh

10) **confundido** (confused)
kohn-foon-DEE-doh

11) **enfermo** (sick)
ehn-FEHR-moh

12) **pícaro/travieso** (naughty)
PEE-kah-roh/trah-VYEH-soh

13) **serio** (serious)
SEH-ryoh

14) **concentrado** (focused)
kohn-sehn-TRAH-doh

15) **aburrido** (bored)
ah-boo-RREE-doh

16) **abrumado** (overwhelmed)
ah-broo-MAH-doh

17) **enamorado** (in love)
eh-nah-moh-RAH-doh

18) **avergonzado/apenado** (ashamed)
ah-vehr-gohn-SAH-doh/ah-peh-NAH-doh

19) **ansioso** (anxious)
ahn-SYOH-soh

20) **asqueado** (disgusted)
ahs-keh-AH-doh

21) **ofendido** (offended)
oh-fehn-DEE-doh

22) **adolorido** (sore)
ah-doh-loh-REE-doh

Te veías muy preocupado en el trabajo.
You looked very worried at work.

Siempre fui muy curioso en la escuela.
I was always very curious at school.

Ella no es muy feliz aquí.
She is not very happy here.

Estoy ansioso por llegar a la fiesta.
I am looking forward to getting to the party.

LA FAMILIA (THE FAMILY)

1) **abuelos** (grandparents)
   ah-BWEH-lohs

2) **abuela** (grandmother)
   ah-BWEH-lah

3) **abuelo** (grandfather)
   ah-BWEH-loh

4) **tío** (uncle)
   TEE-oh

5) **madre** (mother)
   MAH-dreh

6) **padre** (father)
   PAH-dreh

7) **tía** (aunt)
   TEE-ah

8) **primo** (cousin)
   PREE-moh

9) **hermano** (brother)
   ehr-MAH-noh

10) **yo** (me)
    yoh

11) **esposo/a** (husband/wife)
    ehs-POH-soh/sah

12) **hermana** (sister)
    ehr-MAH-nah

13) **prima** (cousin)
    PREE-mah

14) **sobrino** (nephew)
    soh-BREE-noh.

15) **hijo** (son)
    EE-hoh

16) **hija** (daughter)
    EE-hah

17) **sobrina** (niece)
    soh-BREE-nah

18) **nieto** (grandson)
    NYEH-toh

19) **nieta** (granddaughter)
    NYEH-tah

20) **primo segundo** (second cousin)
    PREE-moh seh-GOON-doh

- **Familia Política (In-laws)**
  – Parientes (Relatives)

  fah-MEE-lyah poh-LEE-tee-kah
  pah-ree-EHN-tehs

21) **suegro** (father-in-law)
    SWEH-groh

22) **suegra** (mother-in-law)
    SWEH-grah

23) **cuñado** (brother-in-law)
    koo-NYAH-doh

24) **cuñada** (sister-in-law)
    koo-NYAH-dah

25) **nuera** (daughter-in-law)
    NWEH-rah

26) **yerno** (son-in-law)
    YEHR-noh

27) **tío político** (uncle-in-law)
    TEE-oh poh-LEE-tee-koh

28) **tía política** (aunt-in-law)
    TEE-ah poh-LEE-tee-kah

Los abuelos cuentan las mejores historias.
Grandparents tell the best stories.

Mi padre me da consejos todos los días.
My father gives me advice every day.

Tu suegro es el alma de las fiestas.
Your father-in law is the life of the party.

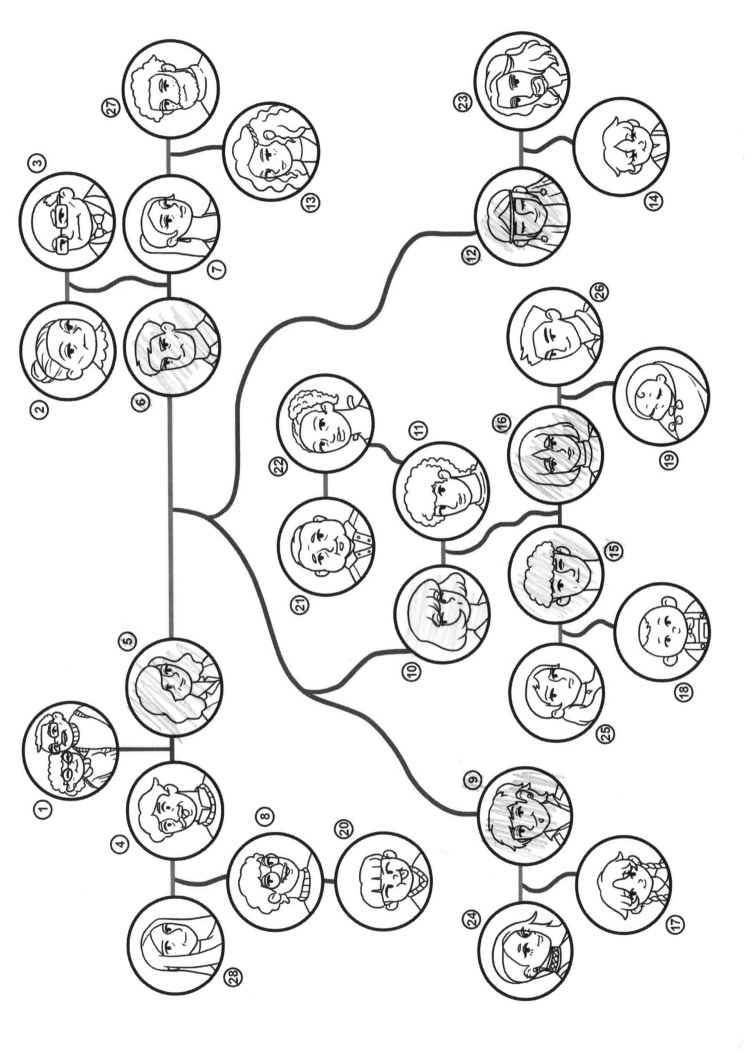

RELACIONES (RELATIONSHIPS)

1) **pareja casada** (married couple)
   pah-REH-hah kah-SAH-dah

2) **casado** (married man)
   kah-SAH-doh

3) **casada** (married woman)
   kah-SAH-dah

4) **pareja divorciada** (divorced couple)
   pah-REH-hah dee-vohr-SYAH-dah

5) **exesposa** (ex-wife)
   ehks-ehs-POH-sah

6) **exesposo** (ex-husband)
   ehks-ehs-POH-soh

7) **amigo/amiga** (friend)
   ah-MEE-goh/ah-MEE-gah

8) **novia** (girlfriend)
   NOH-vyah

9) **novio** (boyfriend)
   NOH-vyoh

10) **vecino/vecina** (neighbor)
    veh-SEE-noh/veh-SEE-nah

11) **soltera/soltero** (single)
    sohl-TEH-rah/sohl-TEH-roh

12) **divorciada/divorciado**
    (divorcée/divorcé)
    dee-vohr-SYAH-dah/dee-vohr-SYAH-doh

13) **viudo** (widower)
    VYOO-doh

14) **viuda** (widow)
    VYOO-dah

Tengo años sin ver a mi exesposo.
I have not seen my ex-husband in years.

La vecina siempre me saluda por la mañana.
My neighbor always greets me in the morning.

Estoy soltero desde hace años.
I have been single for years.

Soy una mujer divorciada e independiente.
I am a divorced and independent woman.

La hermana de su mamá es viuda.
His mother's sister is a widow.

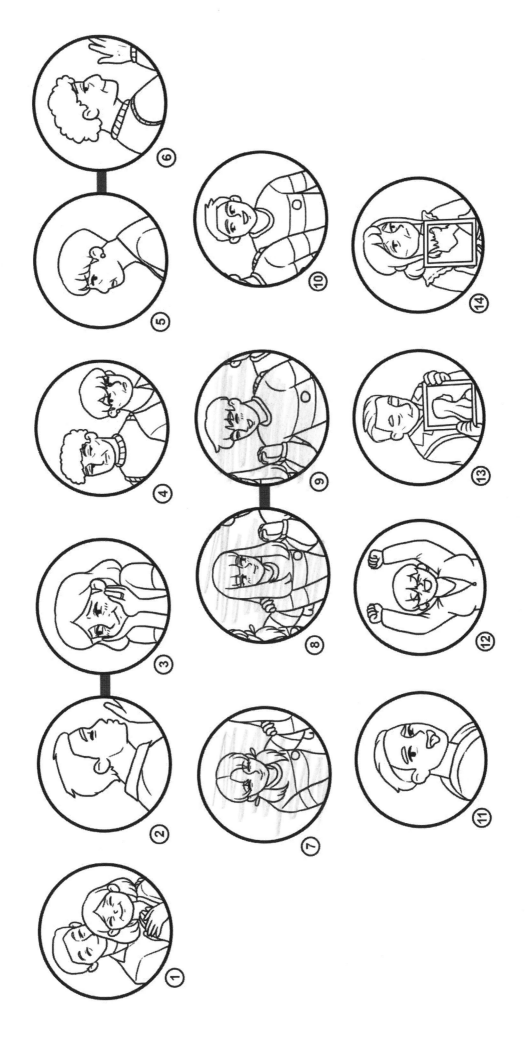

VALORES (VALUES)

1) **respeto** (respect)
rrehs-PEH-toh

2) **gratitud** (gratitude)
grah-tee-TOOD

3) **tolerancia** (tolerance)
toh-leh-RAHN-syah

4) **colaboración** (collaboration)
koh-lah-boh-rah-SYOHN

5) **honestidad** (honesty)
oh-nehs-tee-DAHD

6) **templanza** (temperance)
tehm-PLAHN-sah

7) **responsabilidad** (responsibility)
rrehs-pohn-sah-bee-lee-DAHD

8) **fe** (faith)
feh

9) **coraje/valentía** (courage)
koh-RAH-heh/vah-lehn-TEE-ah

10) **bondad** (kindness)
bohn-DAHD

11) **compromiso** (commitment)
kohm-proh-MEE-soh

12) **entusiasmo** (enthusiasm)
ehn-too-SYAHS-moh

13) **confianza** (trust)
kohn-FYAHN-sah

14) **puntualidad** (punctuality)
poon-twah-lee-DAHD

Siempre trato de mostrar gratitud.
I always try to show gratitude.

Tolerancia es lo que hace falta hoy en día.
Tolerance is what is lacking nowadays.

Mi equipo necesita saber lo que es la colaboración.
My team needs to know what collaboration is.

Siempre cuento con la fe cuando no queda nada más.
I always count on faith when there is nothing left.

Sin entusiasmo no lograremos nada en la vida.
Without enthusiasm, we will achieve nothing in life.

La confianza es algo que puedes perder en un abrir y cerrar de ojos.
Confidence is something you can lose in the blink of an eye.

EL CUERPO HUMANO (THE HUMAN BODY)

1) **cabeza** (head)
kah-BEH-sah

2) **cabello** (hair)
kah-BEH-yoh

3) **cara** (face)
KAH-rah

4) **frente** (forehead)
FREHN-teh

5) **oreja** (ear)
oh-REH-hah

6) **ojo** (eye)
OH-hoh

7) **nariz** (nose)
nah-REES

8) **mejilla** (cheek)
meh-HEE-yah

9) **boca** (mouth)
BOH-kah

10) **barbilla/mentón** (chin)
bahr-BEE-yah/mehn-TOHN

11) **cuello** (neck)
KWEH-yoh

12) **espalda** (back)
ehs-PAHL-dah

13) **pecho** (chest)
PEH-choh

14) **hombro** (shoulder)
OHM-broh

15) **brazo** (arm)
BRAH-soh

16) **antebrazo** (forearm)
ahn-teh-BRAH-soh

17) **mano** (hand)
MAH-noh

18) **abdomen** (abdomen)
ahb-DOH-men

19) **cintura** (waist)
seen-TOO-rah

20) **cadera** (hip)
kah-DEH-rah

21) **pierna** (leg)
PYEHR-nah

22) **muslo** (thigh)
MOOS-loh

23) **rodilla** (knee)
rroh-DEE-yah

24) **pantorrilla** (calf)
pahn-toh-RREE-yah

25) **espinilla** (shin)
ehs-pee-NEE-yah

26) **pie** (foot)
pyeh

El cabello me crece muy rápido.
My hair grows very quickly.

Mi ojo derecho ve mejor que el izquierdo.
I see better with my right eye than with my left.

Tengo comezón en la barbilla.
My chin itches.

Mi brazo está quemado por el sol.
My arm is sunburned.

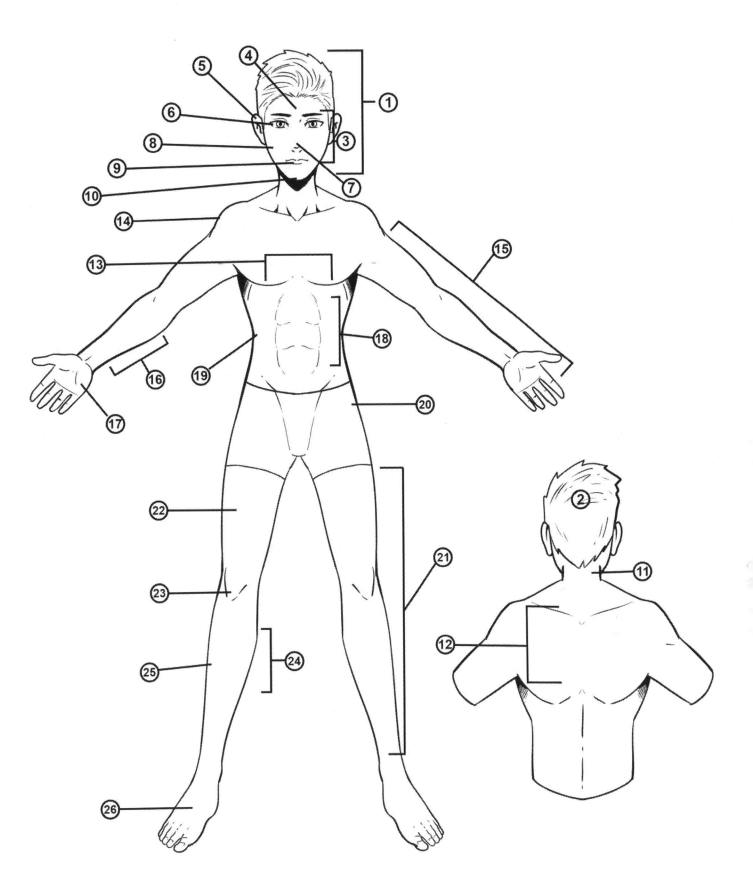

DENTRO DEL CUERPO HUMANO (INSIDE THE HUMAN BODY)

1) **piel** (skin)
   pyehl

2) **músculos** (muscles)
   MOOS-koo-lohs

3) **huesos** (bones)
   WEH-sohs

4) **cerebro** (brain)
   seh-REH-broh

5) **tiroides** (thyroid)
   tee-ROY-dehs

6) **venas** (veins)
   VEH-nahs

7) **arterias** (arteries)
   ahr-TEH-ryahs

8) **corazón** (heart)
   koh-rah-SOHN

9) **pulmones** (lungs)
   pool-MOH-nehs

10) **estómago** (stomach)
    ehs-TOH-mah-goh

11) **esófago** (esophagus)
    eh-SOH-fah-goh

12) **páncreas** (pancreas)
    PAHN-krehahs

13) **hígado** (liver)
    EE-gah-doh

14) **intestino delgado** (small intestine)
    een-tehs-TEE-noh dehl-GAH-doh

15) **intestino grueso** (large intestine)
    een-tehs-TEE-noh GRWEH-soh

16) **vesícula** (gallbladder)
    veh-SEE-koo-lah

17) **riñones** (kidneys)
    rree-NYOH-nehs

18) **vejiga urinaria** (urinary bladder)
    veh-HEE-gah oo-ree-NAH-ryah

La piel es el órgano más grande del cuerpo.
The skin is the largest organ in the body.

La salud de la tiroides es importante para mantener nuestro peso.
Thyroid health is important for maintaining our weight.

Las arterias transportan la sangre del corazón a los tejidos.
Arteries transport blood from the heart to the tissues.

Fumar en exceso afecta los pulmones.
Excess smoking affects the lungs.

El páncreas regula el azúcar de nuestra sangre.
The pancreas regulates the sugar in our blood.

Los riñones remueven toxinas de nuestra sangre.
Kidneys remove toxins from our blood.

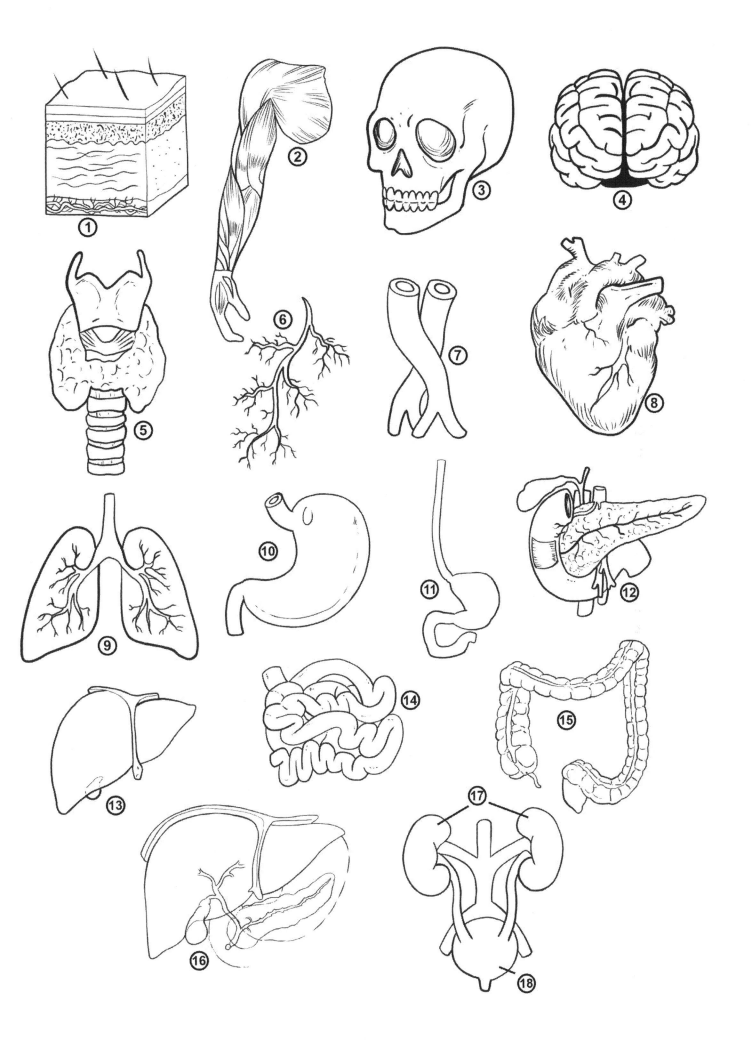

MASCOTAS (PETS)

1) **perro** (dog)
   PEH-rroh
2) **gato** (cat)
   GAH-toh
3) **hurón** (ferret)
   oo-ROHN
4) **mini pig/cerdo tacita de té**
   (mini pig/teacup pig)
   MEE-nee peeg/SEHR-doh tah-SEE-tah
   deh teh
5) **caballo** (horse)
   kah-BAH-yoh
6) **pez ángel** (angelfish)
   pehs AHN-hel
7) **pez payaso** (clown fish)
   pehs pah-YAH-soh
8) **pez dorado** (goldfish)
   pehs doh-RAH-doh
9) **hámster** (hamster)
   HAHMS-tehr
10) **cobaya/conejillo de indias**
    (guinea pig)
    koh-BAH-yah/koh-neh-HEE-yoh deh
    EEN-dyahs

11) **ratón** (mouse)
    rrah-TOHN
12) **conejo** (rabbit)
    koh-NEH-hoh
13) **erizo** (hedgehog)
    eh-REE-soh
14) **tarántula** (tarantula)
    tah-RAHN-too-lah
15) **colonia de hormigas** (ant colony)
    koh-LOH-nyah deh ohr-MEE-gahs
16) **tortuga** (tortoise)
    tohr-TOO-gah
17) **serpiente** (snake)
    sehr-PYEHN-teh
18) **camaleón** (chameleon)
    kah-mah-leh-OHN
19) **iguana** (iguana)
    ee-GWAH-nah
20) **canario** (canary)
    kah-NAH-ryoh
21) **loro/papagayo** (parrot)
    LOH-roh/pah-pah-GAH-yoh
22) **periquito** (parakeet)
    peh-ree-KEE-toh

La serpiente tentó a Eva.
The snake tempted Eve.

Mi perro no muerde.
My dog does not bite.

Soy alérgico al pelo de gato.
I am allergic to cat hair.

Las carreras de caballos son muy buenas por aquí.
The horse races are very good around here.

Quise un hurón, pero mi hermana quiso un gato.
I wanted a ferret, but my sister wanted a cat.

EL ZOOLÓGICO (THE ZOO)

1) **elefante** (elephant)
eh-leh-FAHN-teh

2) **rinoceronte** (rhino)
rree-noh-seh-ROHN-teh

3) **jirafa** (giraffe)
hee-RAH-fah

4) **cebra** (zebra)
SEH-brah

5) **hipopótamo** (hippopotamus)
ee-poh-POH-tah-moh

6) **guepardo** (cheetah)
geh-PAHR-doh

7) **tigre** (tiger)
TEE-greh

8) **león** (lion)
leh-OHN

9) **chimpancé** (chimpanzee)
cheem-pahn-SEH

10) **orangután** (orangutan)
oh-rahng-goo-TAHN

11) **mandril** (baboon)
mahn-DREEL

12) **canguro** (kangaroo)
kahng-GOO-roh

13) **koala** (koala)
koh-AH-lah

14) **lémur** (lemur)
LEH-moor

Los tigres, guepardos y leones son gatos grandes.
Tigers, cheetahs, and lions are big cats.

Los canguros y los koalas son de Australia.
Kangaroos and koalas are from Australia.

Los lémures, los mandriles y los orangutanes son primates.
Lemurs, baboons, and orangutans are primates.

AVES (BIRDS)

1) **avestruz** (ostrich)
ah-vehs-TROOS

2) **pavo real** (peacock)
PAH-voh rreh-AHL

3) **pavo** (turkey)
PAH-voh

4) **gallo** (rooster)
GAH-yoh

5) **pato** (duck)
PAH-toh

6) **cisne** (swan)
SEES-neh

7) **pelícano** (pelican)
peh-LEE-kah-noh

8) **flamenco** (flamingo)
flah-MEHN-koh

9) **paloma** (pigeon)
pah-LOH-mah

10) **búho** (owl)
BOO-oh

11) **buitre** (vulture)
BWEE-treh

12) **águila** (eagle)
AH-gee-lah

13) **gaviota** (seagull)
gah-VYOH-tah

14) **cuervo** (crow)
KWEHR-voh

15) **tucán** (toucan)
too-KAHN

16) **pingüino** (penguin)
peeng-GWEE-noh

17) **pájaro carpintero** (woodpecker)
PAH-hah-roh kahr-peen-TEH-roh

18) **guacamayo/guacamaya** (macaw)
gwah-kah-MAH-yoh

19) **colibrí** (hummingbird)
koh-lee-BREE

20) **kiwi** (kiwi)
KEE-wee

Los búhos, pájaros carpinteros, pavos reales y colibríes eran visitantes comunes donde yo crecí.
Owls, woodpeckers, peacocks, and hummingbirds were common visitors where I grew up.

Vimos unos pelícanos y muchas gaviotas en la playa.
We saw a few pelicans and many seagulls at the beach.

QUIZ #1

Use arrows to match the corresponding translations:

a. nose	1. cerebro
b. baboon	2. asustado
c. concerned	3. tío
d. trust	4. honestidad
e. brain	5. mandril
f. cousin	6. pecho
g. turkey	7. amigo / amiga
h. friend	8. nariz
i. horse	9. huesos
j. scared	10. tigre
k. tiger	11. preocupado
l. bones	12. perro
m. uncle	13. caballo
n. dog	14. primo / prima
o. chest	15. confianza
p. honesty	16. pavo

Fill in the blank spaces with the options below (use each word only once):

Andrea estaba alimentando a su _____, Kif, el sábado en la mañana, antes de ir a casa de su _____. Él no quería comer y se veía _____, tenía los ojos _____, así que lo llevó al veterinario. Allí le revisaron el _____ y vieron que se había tragado ¡un _____ de juguete! Tuvieron que hacerle una cirugía de emergencia, pero todo salió bien, Kif es tan fuerte como un _____. Andrea se sintió muy _____, aunque no pudo ir a ver a sus _____. Lo único bueno fue que evitó que le preguntaran otra vez por qué sigue _____; ella no se siente lista para ese _____, pues sabe que es una gran _____.

soltera

enfermo

responsabilidad

feliz

abuela

compromiso

león

canario

abuelos

gato

tristes

estómago

REPTILES Y ANFIBIOS (REPTILES AND AMPHIBIANS)

- **Reptiles (Reptiles)**
  rehp-TEE-lehs

1) **anaconda** (anaconda)
   ah-nah-KOHN-dah

2) **cobra real** (king cobra)
   KOH-brah rreh-AHL

3) **serpiente de cascabel** (rattlesnake)
   sehr-PYEHN-teh deh kahs-kah-BEHL

4) **serpiente de coral** (coral snake)
   sehr-PYEHN-teh deh koh-RAHL

5) **lagarto cornudo** (horned lizard)
   lah-GAHR-toh kohr-NOO-doh

6) **lagarto de cuello con volantes** (frill-necked lizard)
   lah-GAHR-toh deh KWEH-yoh kohn voh-LAHN-tehs

7) **basilisco común/lagarto Jesucristo** (common basilisk/Jesus Christ lizard)
   bah-see-LEES-koh koh-MOON/lah-GAHR-toh HEH-soo-KREES-toh

8) **dragón de Komodo** (Komodo dragon)
   drah-GOHN deh koh-MOH-doh

9) **cocodrilo** (crocodile)
   koh-koh-DREE-loh

10) **gavial** (gharial/gavial)
    gah-VYAHL

11) **tortuga marina** (sea turtle)
    tohr-TOO-gah mah-REE-nah

- **Anfibios (Amphibians)**
  ahn-FEE-byohs

12) **salamandra** (salamander)
    sah-lah-MAHN-drah

13) **rana Goliat** (Goliath frog)
    RRAH-nah goh-LYAHT

Mis animales favoritos del zoológico fueron la anaconda y la cobra real, pero mi hermana solo quería ver las salamandras y las tortugas marinas.

My favorite animals at the zoo were the anaconda and the king cobra, but my sister only wanted to see the salamanders and sea turtles.

El gavial es muy parecido al cocodrilo.

The gharial is very similar to the crocodile.

INSECTOS Y ARÁCNIDOS (INSECTS AND ARACHNIDS)

- **Insectos (Insects)**
  een-SEHK-tohs

1) **abeja** (bee)
   ah-BEH-hah

2) **abejorro** (bumblebee)
   ah-beh-HOH-rroh

3) **avispa** (wasp)
   ah-VEES-pah

4) **escarabajo** (beetle)
   ehs-kah-rah-BAH-hoh

5) **mariposa** (butterfly)
   mah-ree-POH-sah

6) **polilla** (moth)
   poh-LEE-yah

7) **libélula** (dragonfly)
   lee-BEH-loo-lah

8) **mariquita** (ladybug)
   mah-ree-KEE-tah

9) **luciérnaga** (firefly)
   loo-SYEHR-nah-gah

10) **cucaracha** (cockroach)
    koo-kah-RAH-chah

11) **tábano** (horsefly)
    TAH-bah-noh

12) **mosca** (fly)
    MOHS-kah

13) **mosquito/zancudo** (mosquito)
    mohs-KEE-toh/sahn-KOO-doh

14) **saltamontes** (grasshopper)
    sahl-tah-MOHN-tehs

15) **grillo** (cricket)
    GREE-yoh

- **Arácnidos (Arachnids)**
  ah-RAHK-nee-dohs

16) **escorpión** (scorpion)
    ehs-kohr-PYOHN

17) **araña** (spider)
    ah-RAH-nyah

18) **araña viuda negra** (Southern black widow)
    ah-RAH-nyah VYOO-dah NEH-grah

La mayoría de la gente dice que las mariposas son bonitas, pero que las polillas no lo son.
Most people say that butterflies are beautiful, but that moths are not.

El tipo de insecto más común en el mundo es el escarabajo.
The most common type of insect in the world is the beetle.

Las abejas son pacíficas cuando no se les molesta, pero las avispas picarán sin provocación.
Bees are peaceful when not bothered, but wasps will sting without provocation.

La mayoría de las arañas son inofensivas, pero la picadura de una viuda negra puede ser mortal en algunos casos.
Most spiders are harmless, but the bite from a black widow can be fatal in some cases.

MAMÍFEROS I (MAMMALS I)

1) **murciélago** (bat)
   moor-SYEH-lah-goh

2) **ornitorrinco** (platypus)
   ohr-nee-toh-RREEN-koh

3) **ballena asesina/orca** (killer whale/orca)
   bah-YEH-nah ah-seh-SEE-nah/OHR-kah

4) **delfín** (dolphin)
   dehl-FEEN

5) **castor** (beaver)
   kahs-TOHR

6) **marmota** (groundhog)
   mahr-MOH-tah

7) **topo** (mole)
   TOH-poh

8) **ardilla** (squirrel)
   ahr-DEE-yah

9) **comadreja** (weasel)
   koh-mah-DREH-hah

10) **zarigüeya** (possum/opossum)
    sah-ree-GWEH-yah

11) **rata** (rat)
    RRAH-tah

12) **liebre** (hare)
    LYEH-breh

13) **tejón** (badger)
    teh-HOHN

14) **zorrillo/mofeta** (skunk)
    soh-RREE-yoh/moh-FEH-tah

15) **leopardo** (leopard)
    leh-oh-PAHR-doh

Si la marmota ve su sombra, habrá seis semanas más de invierno.
If the groundhog sees his shadow, there will be six more weeks of winter.

Los delfines y las orcas pueden ser tan inteligentes como los humanos.
Dolphins and killer whales may be as smart as humans.

Las zarigüeyas son animales beneficiosos que comen garrapatas y otros insectos.
Possums are beneficial animals that eat ticks and other insects.

El castor es el animal oficial de Canadá.
The beaver is the official animal of Canada.

MAMÍFEROS II (MAMMALS II)

1) **oso** (bear)
   OH-soh

2) **hiena** (hyena)
   YEH-nah

3) **chacal** (jackal)
   chah-KAHL

4) **vaca** (cow)
   VAH-kah

5) **toro** (bull)
   TOH-roh

6) **zorro** (fox)
   SOH-rroh

7) **búfalo** (buffalo)
   BOO-fah-loh

8) **alce** (elk/moose)
   AHL-seh

9) **oveja** (sheep)
   oh-VEH-hah

10) **cabra** (goat)
    KAH-brah

11) **gacela** (gazelle)
    gah-SEH-lah

12) **lobo** (wolf)
    LOH-boh

13) **mono** (monkey)
    MOH-noh

14) **carnero** (ram)
    kahr-NEH-roh

15) **burro/asno** (donkey)
    BOO-rroh/AHS-noh

De niño vi alces, lobos y búfalos silvestres en nuestras vacaciones familiares.
As a child, I saw wild moose, wolves, and buffaloes on our family vacations.

Algunos depredadores de las gacelas son las hienas, guepardos, leopardos y chacales.
Some of the gazelle's predators are hyenas, cheetahs, leopards, and jackals.

PECES Y MOLUSCOS (FISH AND MOLLUSKS)

- **Peces (Fish)**
  PEH-sehs

1) **tiburón ballena** (whale shark)
   tee-boo-ROHN bah-YEH-nah

2) **tiburón blanco** (white shark)
   tee-boo-ROHN BLAHN-koh

3) **tiburón martillo** (hammerhead shark)
   tee-boo-ROHN mahr-TEE-yoh

4) **pez espada** (swordfish/marlin)
   pehs ehs-PAH-dah

5) **barracuda** (barracuda)
   bah-rrah-KOO-dah

6) **pez globo** (pufferfish)
   pehs GLOH-boh

7) **bagre/pez gato** (catfish)
   BAH-greh/pehs GAH-toh

8) **piraña** (piranha)
   pee-RAH-nyah

9) **pez volador** (flying fish)
   pehs voh-lah-DOHR

10) **morena** (moray eel)
    moh-REH-nah

11) **mantarraya** (manta ray)
    mahn-tah-RRAH-yah

12) **caballito de mar/hipocampo** (seahorse)
    kah-bah-YEE-toh deh mahr/ee-poh-KAHM-poh

- **Moluscos (Mollusks)**
  moh-LOOS-kohs

13) **calamar** (squid)
    kah-lah-MAHR

14) **sepia** (cuttlefish)
    SEH-pyah

15) **pulpo** (octopus)
    POOL-poh

16) **ostra** (oyster)
    OHS-trah

17) **almeja** (clam)
    ahl-MEH-hah

18) **nautilo** (nautilus)
    NOW-tee-loh

19) **caracol** (snail)
    kah-rah-KOHL

20) **babosa** (slug)
    bah-BOH-sah

El restaurante sirve pez espada, tiburón blanco y ostras, pero no tiene pez globo.
The restaurant serves swordfish, white shark, and oysters, but it does not have pufferfish.

La mejor parte del viaje fue ver la mantarraya y el pez volador.
The best part of the trip was seeing the manta ray and the flying fish.

Me gusta la mayoría de los moluscos, pero no comeré caracoles.
I like most mollusks, but I will not eat snails.

ROPA I (CLOTHING I)

1) **impermeable** (raincoat)
eem-pehr-meh-AH-bleh

2) **sudadera** (hoodie)
soo-dah-DEH-rah

3) **chaqueta** (jacket)
chah-KEH-tah

4) **jeans/vaqueros** (jeans)
jeens/vah-KEH-rohs

5) **boxers/calzoncillos tipo bóxer** (boxer shorts)
BOHK-sehrs/kahl-sohn-SEE-yohs TEE-poh BOHK-sehr

6) **botas** (boots)
BOH-tahs

7) **pendientes/aretes/zarcillos** (earrings)
pehn-DYEHN-tehs/ah-REH-tehs/sahr-SEE-yohs

8) **suéter/sudadera** (sweater)
SWEH-tehr/soo-dah-DEH-rah

9) **collar** (necklace)
koh-YAHR

10) **sostén/brasier** (bra)
sohs-TEHN/brah-SYEHR

11) **leggings/mallas** (leggings)
LEH-geengs/MAH-yahs

12) **medias/calcetines** (socks)
MEH-dyahs/kahl-seh-TEE-nehs

13) **blusa** (blouse/top)
BLOO-sah

14) **brazalete/pulsera** (bracelet)
brah-sah-LEH-teh/pool-SEH-rah

15) **shorts/pantalones cortos** (shorts)
shorts/pahn-tah-LOH-nehs KOHR-tohs

16) **panties/bragas** (panties)
PAHN-tees/BRAH-gahs

17) **abrigo** (coat)
ah-BREE-goh

18) **vestido** (dress)
vehs-TEE-doh

19) **cartera/bolsa** (purse)
kahr-TEH-rah/BOHL-sah

20) **sandalias** (sandals)
sahn-DAH-lyahs

Estoy buscando un collar y aretes para combinar con este vestido.
I am looking for a necklace and earrings to go with this dress.

Las sandalias con shorts no se ven bien.
Sandals with shorts does not look good.

Bastará con un suéter o una chaqueta ligera; no está lo bastante frío como para un abrigo.
A light sweater or a jacket will do; it is not cold enough for a coat.

ROPA II (CLOTHING II)

1) **sombrero** (hat)
sohm-BREH-roh

2) **esmoquin** (tuxedo/smoking)
ehs-MOH-keen

3) **pajarita/corbata de lazo/corbatín** (bow tie)
pah-hah-REE-tah/kohr-BAH-tah deh LAH-soh/kohr-bah-TEEN

4) **zapatos** (shoes)
sah-PAH-tohs

5) **traje** (suit)
TRAH-heh

6) **camisa** (shirt)
kah-MEE-sah

7) **corbata** (tie)
kohr-BAH-tah

8) **maletín** (briefcase/case)
mah-leh-TEEN

9) **blusa de manga larga** (long-sleeved blouse)
BLOO-sah deh MAHN-gah LAHR-gah

10) **sostén deportivo** (sports bra)
sohs-TEHN deh-pohr-TEE-voh

11) **pantalones** (trousers/pants)
pahn-tah-LOH-nehs

12) **cinturón** (belt)
seen-too-ROHN

13) **anillo** (ring)
ah-NEE-yoh

14) **playera/camiseta** (T-shirt)
plah-YEH-rah/kah-mee-SEH-tah

15) **falda** (skirt)
FAHL-dah

16) **bufanda** (scarf)
boo-FAHN-dah

17) **reloj** (watch)
rreh-LOHH

18) **pantalones cargo** (cargo pants)
pahn-tah-LOH-nehs KAHR-goh

19) **billetera** (wallet)
bee-yeh-TEH-rah

20) **paraguas/sombrilla** (umbrella)
pah-RAH-gwahs/sohm-BREE-yah

Rara vez me pongo un traje, pero jamás me verás en esmoquin.
I rarely put on a suit, but you will never see me in a tuxedo.

Ella no usa anillo o reloj, ya que la joyería le incomoda.
She does not wear a ring or a watch, since jewelry makes her uncomfortable.

EL CLIMA (THE WEATHER)

1) **soleado** (sunny)
soh-leh-AH-doh

2) **caliente** (hot)
kah-LYEHN-teh

3) **tormenta de arena** (sandstorm)
tohr-MEHN-tah deh ah-REH-nah

4) **nublado** (cloudy)
noo-BLAH-doh

5) **cálido** (warm)
KAH-lee-doh

6) **nublado/brumoso** (foggy/misty)
noo-BLAH-doh/broo-MOH-soh

7) **lluvioso** (rainy)
yoo-VYOH-soh

8) **fresco** (cool)
FREHS-koh

9) **gota de lluvia** (raindrop)
GOH-tah deh YOO-vyah

10) **húmedo** (humid)
OO-meh-doh

11) **tormenta** (storm)
tohr-MEHN-tah

12) **rayo/relámpago** (lightning)
RRAH-yoh/rreh-LAHM-pah-goh

13) **ventoso** (windy)
vehn-TOH-soh

14) **nevado** (snowy)
neh-VAH-doh

15) **frío** (cold)
FREE-oh

16) **copo de nieve** (snowflake)
KOH-poh deh NYEH-eh

Prefiero los días lluviosos a los soleados porque no me gusta el clima cálido.
I prefer rainy days over sunny days because I do not like warm weather.

Es bastante cálido en la tarde, pero fresco en la noche.
It is quite warm in the afternoon, but it's cool in the evening.

Hubo una tormenta con rayos, así que no pude dormir anoche.
There was a storm with lightning, so I could not sleep last night.

LAS ESTACIONES – PRIMAVERA (THE SEASONS – SPRING)

1) **jardín** (garden)
   hahr-DEEN

2) **flor/florecimiento** (blossom)
   flohr/floh-reh-see-MYEHN-toh

3) **picnic** (picnic)
   PIHK-neek

4) **parque** (park)
   PAHR-keh

5) **paseo en bicicleta** (bike ride)
   pah-SEH-oh ehn bee-see-KLEH-tah

6) **limonada** (lemonade)
   lee-moh-NAH-dah

7) **venta de cochera/garaje** (garage sale)
   VEHN-tah deh koh-CHEH-rah/gah-RAH-heh

8) **viaje por carretera** (roadtrip)
   VYAH-heh pohr kah-rreh-TEH-rah

9) **pintar rocas** (to paint rocks)
   peen-TAHR RROH-kahs

10) **plantar algunas flores** (to plant some flowers)
    plahn-TAHR ahl-GOO-nahs FLOH-rehs

11) **volar una cometa** (to fly a kite)
    voh-LAHR OO-nah koh-MEH-tah

12) **asistir a una barbacoa** (to attend a barbecue)
    ah-sees-TEER ah OO-nah bahr-bah-KOH-ah

Tuvimos una venta de cochera para recaudar fondos para nuestro viaje por carretera.
We had a garage sale to raise money for our roadtrip.

Tuvieron un picnic en el parque, y los niños volaron una cometa.
They had a picnic in the park, and the kids flew a kite.

Plantamos algunas flores la semana pasada y vimos los primeros florecimientos esta mañana.
We planted some flowers last week and saw the first blossoms this morning.

LAS ESTACIONES – VERANO (THE SEASONS – SUMMER)

1) **ir a acampar** (to go camping)
eer ah ah-kahm-PAHR

2) **parque acuático** (water park)
PAHR-keh ah-KWAH-tee-koh

3) **actividades al aire libre** (outdoor activities)
ahk-tee-vee-DAH-dehs ahl AY-reh LEE-breh

4) **piscina** (swimming pool)
pee-SEE-nah

5) **nadar** (to swim)
nah-DAHR

6) **broncearse** (to get tanned)
brohn-seh-AHR-seh

7) **protector solar** (sunscreen)
proh-tehk-TOHR soh-LAHR

8) **repelente de insectos** (insect repellent)
rreh-peh-LEHN-teh deh een-SEHK-tohs

9) **lago** (lake)
LAH-goh

10) **salvavidas** (lifesaver/lifeguard)
sahl-vah-VEE-dahs

11) **castillo de arena** (sandcastle)
kahs-TEE-yoh deh ah-REH-nah

12) **ir a una caminata** (to go on a hike)
eer ah OO-nah kah-mee-NAH-tah

Aun si quieres broncearte, debes usar protector solar si vas a nadar en la piscina.
Even if you want to get tanned, you should wear sunscreen if you are going to swim in the pool.

Fueron a una caminata, pero se les olvidó llevar repelente de insectos, y por eso tuvieron que regresar.
They went on a hike, but forgot to take insect repellent, and so they had to turn back.

QUIZ #2

Use arrows to match the corresponding translations:

a. roadtrip

b. rattlesnake

c. storm

d. cow

e. shoes

f. wasp

g. swimming pool

h. dolphin

i. coat

j. squid

k. beetle

l. scarf

m. sheep

n. dress

o. beaver

p. sandcastle

1. abrigo

2. bufanda

3. delfín

4. castor

5. tormenta

6. oveja

7. castillo de arena

8. vestido

9. escarabajo

10. viaje por carretera

11. zapatos

12. piscina

13. vaca

14. serpiente de cascabel

15. calamar

16. avispa

Fill in the blank spaces with the options below (use each word only once):

Durante la primavera mi familia y yo solemos ir a _____ al bosque. Siempre llevamos ropa cómoda, como _____, y el _____ no puede faltar para alejar a las _____ y los _____. Me encanta _____ con mi hermano, incluso si el clima está _____. A veces, me da miedo encontrarme con un _____, un _____ o un _____, pero mamá dice que no viven en esa zona. Al volver a casa cenaremos un delicioso _____, es la especialidad de papá en la cocina, tomaremos _____ y nos reiremos de todo lo que sucedió en el viaje.

cocodrilo

moscas

oso

ir a una caminata

lluvioso

pantalones cargo

limonada

leopardo

plantar algunas flores

bagre / pez gato

repelente de insectos

mosquitos

LAS ESTACIONES – OTOÑO (THE SEASONS – FALL/AUTUMN)

1) **hojas cambiando de color** (changing leaves)
OH-hahs kahm-BYAHN-doh deh koh-LOHR

2) **recoger hojas** (to collect leaves)
rreh-koh-HEHR OH-hahs

3) **calabaza** (pumpkin)
kah-lah-BAH-sah

4) **tallar calabazas** (to carve pumpkins)
tah-YAHR kah-lah-BAH-sahs

5) **recolección/recogida de manzanas** (apple picking)
rreh-koh-lehk-SYOHN deh mahn-SAH-nahs

6) **disfraz de Halloween** (Halloween costume)
dees-FRAHS deh HAH-loh-ween

7) **dulces de Halloween** (Halloween candy)
DOOL-sehs deh HAH-loh-ween

8) **velas aromáticas** (spiced candles)
VEH-lahs ah-roh-MAH-tee-kahs

9) **cena de Acción de Gracias** (Thanksgiving dinner)
SEH-nah deh ahk-SYOHN deh GRAH-syahs

10) **manta de lana/cobija de lana** (wool blanket)
MAHN-tah deh LAH-nah/koh-BEE-hah deh LAH-nah

11) **asar malvaviscos** (to roast marshmallows)
ah-SAHR mahl-vah-VEES-kohs

12) **decorar el patio** (to decorate the yard)
deh-koh-RAHR ehl PAH-tyoh

En el otoño, a Susan le encanta recoger hojas y decorar el patio, pero a Katherine solo le interesan los dulces de Halloween.
In the autumn, Susan loves collecting leaves and decorating the yard, but Katherine is only interested in Halloween candy.

No me gusta ninguna comida servida en la cena de Acción de Gracias.
I do not like any of the food served at Thanksgiving dinner.

Asamos malvaviscos durante dos semanas.
We roasted marshmallows for two weeks.

LAS ESTACIONES – INVIERNO (THE SEASONS – WINTER)

1) **chocolate caliente** (hot cocoa/hot chocolate)
choh-koh-LAH-teh kah-LYEHN-teh

2) **trineo** (sled)
tree-NEH-oh

3) **guantes/manoplas** (mittens)
GWAHN-tehs/mah-NOH-plahs

4) **chaqueta acolchada/chaqueta esponjosa** (puffy jacket)
chah-KEH-tah ah-kohl-CHAH-dah/chah-KEH-tah ehs-pohn-HOH-sah

5) **sopa** (soup)
SOH-pah

6) **galletas de jengibre** (gingerbread cookies)
gah-YEH-tahs deh hehn-HEE-breh

7) **ventana helada** (frosty window)
vehn-TAH-nah eh-LAH-dah

8) **fruto del pino/piña de pino** (pinecone)
FROO-toh dehl PEE-noh/PEE-nyah deh PEE-noh

9) **patinaje sobre hielo** (ice skating)
pah-tee-NAH-heh SOH-breh YEH-loh

10) **esquí** (ski)
ehs-KEE

11) **pista de hielo** (ice rink)
PEES-tah deh YEH-loh

12) **bola de nieve** (snowball)
BOH-lah deh NYEH-veh

A mi esposa le gusta el patinaje sobre hielo, pero yo prefiero quedarme en la cabaña comiendo galletas de jenjibre, tomando chocolate caliente y mirando por la ventana helada.
My wife likes ice skating, but I prefer to stay in the cabin eating gingerbread cookies, drinking hot chocolate and looking out the frosty window.

EL TIEMPO (TIME)

1) **huso horario** (time zone)
   OO-soh oh-RAH-ryoh

2) **segundo** (second)
   seh-GOON-doh

3) **minuto** (minute)
   mee-NOO-toh

4) **hora** (hour)
   OH-rah

5) **día** (day)
   DEE-ah

6) **semana** (week)
   seh-MAH-nah

7) **quincena** (fortnight)
   keen-SEH-nah

8) **mes** (month)
   mehs

9) **año** (year)
   AH-nyoh

10) **amanecer** (dawn)
    ah-mah-neh-SEHR

11) **mañana** (morning)
    mah-NYAH-nah

12) **mediodía** (noon/midday)
    meh-dyoh-DEE-ah

13) **tarde** (afternoon)
    TAHR-deh

14) **atardecer/anochecer** (dusk)
    ah-tahr-deh-SEHR/ah-noh-cheh-SEHR

15) **noche** (night)
    NOH-cheh

16) **medianoche** (midnight)
    meh-dyah-NOH-cheh

17) **fecha** (date)
    FEH-chah

18) **calendario** (calendar)
    kah-lehn-DAH-ryoh

Trabajo desde el anochecer hasta el amanecer.
I work from dusk to dawn.

La mayoría de las empresas pagan cada quincena, así que el banco está muy concurrido dos veces al mes.
Most companies pay every fortnight, so the bank is very busy twice a month.

Es importante prestar atención a los husos horarios al trabajar a nivel internacional.
It is important to pay attention to time zones when working at an international level.

① ③ ④ ②

⑤ TODAY
APRIL
10

MAY 2020

2020						
SUN	MON	TUE	WED	THU	FRI	SAT

⑥

⑦

SUN	MON	TUE	WED	THU	FRI	SAT
2	3	4	5	6	7	8
9	10	11	12	13	14	15

⑧

2020			
JAN	FEB	MARCH	APRIL
MAY	JUNE	JULY	AUG
SEPT	OCT	NOV	DEC

⑨

⑰ MAY 1

⑱ APRIL 2020

SUN	MON	TUE	WED	THU	FRI	SAT

⑩ ⑪ ⑫ ⑬ ⑭ ⑮ ⑯

LA CASA (THE HOUSE)

1) **ático** (attic)
AH-tee-koh

2) **tejado** (roof)
teh-HAH-doh

3) **techo** (ceiling)
TEH-choh

4) **chimenea** (chimney)
chee-meh-NEH-ah

5) **pared** (wall)
pah-REHD

6) **balcón** (balcony)
bahl-KOHN

7) **porche/pórtico** (porch)
POHR-cheh/POHR-tee-koh

8) **ventana** (window)
vehn-TAH-nah

9) **persianas** (shutters)
pehr-SYAH-nahs

10) **puerta** (door)
PWEHR-tah

11) **escaleras** (stairs)
ehs-kah-LEH-rahs

12) **barandilla/pasamanos** (bannister)
bah-rahn-DEE-yah/pah-sah-MAH-nohs

13) **piso** (floor)
PEE-soh

14) **sótano** (basement)
SOH-tah-noh

15) **patio** (backyard)
PAH-tyoh

16) **cochera** (garage)
koh-CHEH-rah

17) **entrada/calzada** (driveway)
ehn-TRAH-dah/kahl-SAH-dah

18) **cerca/reja/verja** (fence/picket fence)
SEHR-kah/RREH-hah/VEHR-hah

19) **buzón de correo** (mailbox)
boo-SOHN deh koh-RREH-oh

20) **pasillo/corredor** (hallway/corridor)
pah-SEE-yoh/koh-rreh-DOHR

Los buzones de correo están en el pasillo, al pie de las escaleras.
The mailboxes are in the hallway, at the foot of the stairs.

Su casa de ensueño tiene un sótano, un patio grande y un porche.
Their dream house has a basement, a large backyard, and a porch.

Al lado de la puerta hay una ventana con persianas.
To the side of the door, there is a window with shutters.

ARTÍCULOS DE COCINA (KITCHEN ITEMS)

1) **estufa/cocina** (stove)
ehs-TOO-fah/koh-SEE-nah

2) **horno de microondas** (microwave oven)
OHR-noh deh mee-kroh-OHN-dahs

3) **horno eléctrico/horno tostador** (toaster oven)
OHR-noh eh-LEHK-tree-koh/OHR-noh tohs-tah-DOHR

4) **batidora eléctrica** (electric mixer)
bah-tee-DOH-rah eh-LEHK-tree-kah

5) **licuadora** (blender)
lee-kwah-DOH-rah

6) **tostadora** (toaster)
tohs-tah-DOH-rah

7) **cafetera** (coffee maker)
kah-feh-TEH-rah

8) **refrigerador** (fridge)
rreh-free-heh-rah-DOHR

9) **despensa** (pantry)
dehs-PEHN-sah

10) **alacena** (cupboard)
ah-lah-SEH-nah

11) **molde para hornear** (cake pan)
MOHL-deh PAH-rah ohr-neh-AHR

12) **sartén** (frying pan)
sahr-TEHN

13) **olla/caldero** (pot)
OH-yah/kahl-DEH-roh

14) **cortadores/moldes de galletas** (cookie cutters)
kohr-tah-DOH-rehs/MOHL-dehs deh gah-YEH-tahs

15) **tazón para mezclar** (mixing bowl)
tah-SOHN PAH-rah mehs-KLAHR

16) **escurridor** (colander)
ehs-koo-rree-DOHR

17) **colador** (strainer)
koh-lah-DOHR

18) **rodillo de amasar** (rolling pin)
rroh-DEE-yoh deh ah-mah-SAHR

19) **guante para horno** (oven mitt)
GWAHN-teh PAH-rah OHR-noh

20) **delantal** (apron)
deh-lahn-TAHL

No tengo horno de microondas; prefiero cocinar en la estufa.
I do not have a microwave; I prefer to cook on the stove.

Una cafetera es tan esencial como un refrigerador.
A coffee maker is as essential as a fridge.

Él compró un tazón para mezclar y moldes de galleta para hornear con los niños.
He bought a mixing bowl and cookie cutters to bake with the kids.

ARTÍCULOS DE HABITACIÓN/ARTÍCULOS DE DORMITORIO (BEDROOM ITEMS)

1) **cama (bed)**
   KAH-mah

2) **colchón** (mattress)
   kohl-CHOHN

3) **ropa de cama** (bedding/bed linen)
   RROH-pah deh KAH-mah

4) **almohada** (pillow)
   ahl-moh-AH-dah

5) **sábana** (sheet)
   SAH-bah-nah

6) **cobija/manta** (blanket)
   koh-BEE-hah/MAHN-tah

7) **cobertor** (spread)
   koh-behr-TOHR

8) **funda de almohada** (pillowcase)
   FOON-dah deh ahl-moh-AH-dah

9) **mesa de noche** (nightstand)
   MEH-sah deh NOH-cheh

10) **reloj de mesa** (table clock)
    rreh-LOHH deh MEH-sah

11) **lámpara de mesa** (table light)
    LAHM-pah-rah deh MEH-sah

12) **clóset/armario** (closet)
    KLOH-seht/ahr-MAH-ryoh

13) **mecedora** (rocking chair)
    meh-seh-DOH-rah

14) **lámpara** (lamp)
    LAHM-pah-rah

15) **espejo** (mirror)
    ehs-PEH-hoh

16) **cómoda** (dresser)
    KOH-moh-dah

17) **cortina** (curtain)
    kohr-TEE-nah

18) **cuna** (cradle/crib)
    KOO-nah

19) **móvil de cuna** (crib mobile)
    MOH-veel deh KOO-nah

20) **percha** (hanger)
    PEHR-chah

Ella cambia la ropa de cama dos veces a la semana.
She changes the bedding twice a week.

Hay un espejo arriba de la cómoda.
There is a mirror above the dresser.

Él se enfría más rápido que ella, así que guarda una cobija extra debajo de la cama.
He gets cold faster than her, so he keeps an extra blanket under the bed.

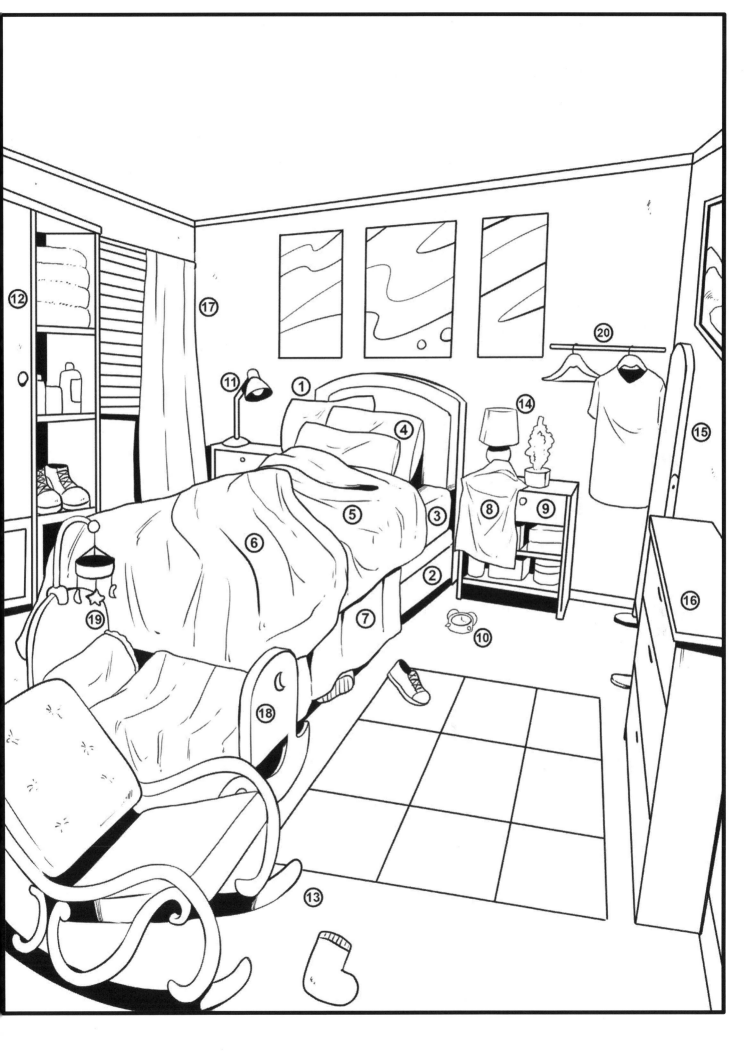

ARTÍCULOS DE BAÑO/ARTÍCULOS DE TOCADOR (BATHROOM ITEMS)

1) **cortina de baño** (shower curtain)
kohr-TEE-nah deh BAH-nyoh

2) **toalla** (towel)
toh-AH-yah

3) **toallero** (towel rack)
toh-ah-YEH-roh

4) **toalla de mano** (hand towel)
toh-AH-yah deh MAH-noh

5) **bañera/tina** (bathtub)
bah-NYEH-rah/TEE-nah

6) **ducha** (shower)
DOO-chah

7) **retrete/inodoro** (toilet/WC)
rreh-TREH-teh/ee-noh-DOH-roh

8) **lavabo/lavamanos** (sink/washbasin)
lah-VAH-boh/lah-vah-MAH-nohs

9) **grifo/llave** (faucet/tap)
GREE-foh/YAH-veh

10) **alfombra de baño** (bathmat)
ahl-FOHM-brah deh BAH-nyoh

11) **gabinete de medicinas** (medicine cabinet)
gah-bee-NEH-teh deh meh-dee-SEE-nahs

12) **dentífrico/pasta dental** (toothpaste)
dehn-TEE-free-koh/PAHS-tah dehn-TAHL

13) **cepillo de dientes** (toothbrush)
seh-PEE-yoh deh DYEHN-tehs

14) **champú** (shampoo)
champ-POO

15) **peine** (comb)
PEY-neh

16) **jabón** (soap)
hah-BOHN

17) **espuma para afeitar** (shaving foam)
ehs-POO-mah deh ah-fey-TAHR

18) **rasuradora/afeitadora** (razor/shaver)
rrah-soo-rah-DOH-rah
ah-fey-tah-DOH-rah

19) **papel higiénico** (toilet paper)
pah-PEHL ee-HYEH-nee-koh

20) **destapacaños/émbolo** (plunger)
dehs-tah-pah-KAH-nyohs/EHM-boh-loh

21) **escobilla para inodoro** (toilet brush)
ehs-koh-BEE-yah PAH-rah ee-noh-DOH-roh

22) **papelera/basurero** (wastebasket)
pah-peh-LEH-rah/bah-soo-REH-roh

Por tu salud, pon tu peine y cepillo de dientes en el gabinete de medicinas.
For your health, put your comb and toothbrush in the medicine cabinet.

Me gusta el lavabo, pero el grifo es demasiado grande.
I like the sink, but the faucet is too big.

Debes lavar tus toallas y alfombras de baño con regularidad.
You should wash your towels and bathmats regularly.

ARTÍCULOS DE SALA (LIVING ROOM ITEMS)

1) **muebles** (furniture)
   MWEH-bleh

2) **silla** (chair)
   SEE-yah

3) **sofa** (sofá)
   soh-FAH

4) **sillón** (couch)
   see-YOHN

5) **cojín** (cushion)
   koh-HEEN

6) **mesita del salón/mesa de centro**
   (coffee table)
   meh-SEE-tah dehl sah-LOHN/MEH-sah deh SEHN-troh

7) **cenicero** (ashtray)
   seh-nee-SEH-roh

8) **florero** (vase)
   floh-REH-roh

9) **adornos** (ornaments)
   ah-DOHR-nohs

10) **estantería/estante**
    (bookshelf/bookcase)
    ehs-tahn-teh-REE-ah/ehs-TAHN-teh

11) **revistero** (magazine holder)
    rreh-vees-TEH-roh

12) **equipo de música** (stereo)
    eh-KEE-poh deh MOO-see-kah

13) **altavoces** (speakers)
    ahl-tah-VOH-sehs

14) **chimenea** (fireplace)
    chee-meh-NEH-ah

15) **candelabro** (chandelier)
    kahn-deh-LAH-broh

16) **lámpara** (lamp)
    LAHM-pah-rah

17) **bombillo/bombilla** (light bulb)
    bohm-BEE-yoh/bohm-BEE-yah

18) **reloj de pared** (wall clock)
    rreh-LOHH deh pah-REHD

19) **cuadro/pintura** (painting)
    KWAH-droh/peen-TOO-rah

20) **televisor/televisión** (TV/television)
    teh-leh-vee-SOHR/teh-leh-vee-SYOHN

21) **control remoto** (remote control)
    kohn-TROHL rreh-MOH-toh

22) **videoconsola/consola de videojuegos**
    (video game console)
    vee-deh-oh-kohn-SOH-lah/kohn-SOH-lah deh vee-deh-oh-HWEH-gohs

Tiene pocos muebles en su sala: solo una silla y una televisión.
He has very little furniture in his living room: only a chair and a television.

¿Podrías recoger unas bombillas para el candelabro y las lámparas?
Could you pick up some light bulbs for the chandelier and the lamps?

Su casa está llena de pinturas y adornos que ella misma hizo.
Her house is filled with paintings and ornaments she made herself.

ARTÍCULOS DE COMEDOR (DINING ROOM ITEMS)

1) **mesa del comedor** (dining table)
MEH-sah dehl koh-meh-DOHR

2) **mantel** (tablecloth)
mahn-TEHL

3) **centro de mesa** (centerpiece)
SEHN-troh deh MEH-sah

4) **mantel individual** (placemat)
mahn-TEHL een-dee-vee-DWAHL

5) **plato** (plate)
PLAH-toh

6) **servilleta** (napkin)
sehr-vee-YEH-tah

7) **cuchillo** (knife)
koo-CHEE-yoh

8) **tenedor** (fork)
teh-neh-DOHR

9) **cuchara** (spoon)
koo-CHAH-rah

10) **jarra** (pitcher/jar)
HAH-rrah

11) **vaso/copa** (glass)
VAH-soh/KOH-pah

12) **taza** (mug/cup)
TAH-sah

13) **salero** (saltshaker)
sah-LEH-roh

14) **pimentero** (pepper shaker)
pee-mehn-TEH-roh

15) **bandeja** (tray)
bahn-DEH-hah

16) **bebida** (drink/beverage)
beh-BEE-dah

17) **comida** (food)
koh-MEE-dah

18) **merienda** (snack)
meh-RYEHN-dah

Ella no pone salero o pimentero en la mesa del comedor, ya que sazona su comida adecuadamente.
She does not put a saltshaker or a pepper shaker on the dining table, as she seasons her food properly.

Solo usan mantel, centro de mesa y manteles individuales cuando hay compañía.
They only use a tablecloth, a centerpiece, and placemats when there is company.

QUIZ #3

Use arrows to match the corresponding translations:

a. week	1. noche
b. pillow	2. delantal
c. toothbrush	3. ventana
d. knife	4. patinaje sobre hielo
e. chair	5. semana
f. pot	6. toalla
g. bed	7. cuchillo
h. couch	8. vaso / copa
i. apron	9. almohada
j. window	10. decorar el patio
k. towel	11. escaleras
l. night	12. cepillo de dientes
m. stairs	13. cama
n. ice skating	14. sillón
o. glass	15. olla / caldero
p. to decorate the yard	16. silla

Fill in the blank spaces with the options below (use each word only once):

David tenía una reunión importante al _____, pero se quedó dormido y se la perdió. Al _____ siguiente invitó a sus socios a una gran _____ para disculparse por haber faltado. David ordenó la mejor _____ que pudo encontrar, ellos dejaron sus autos en la _____, y todos cenaron frente a la _____. Luego, fue al _____ y buscó los ingredientes para preparar un _____, pues comenzaron a tener frío. También buscó unas _____. En ese momento, pasó frente al _____ y se dio cuenta de que tenía una mancha de salsa en el rostro, así que quiso limpiarse con una _____, pero no fue suficiente; fue rápidamente al baño y se limpió con _____, volviendo a la reunión como si nada hubiese pasado para seguir disfrutando de la agradable velada.

chocolate caliente	día
refrigerador	espejo
entrada / calzada	chimenea
mantas de lana / cobijas de lana	servilleta
atardecer	comida
jabón	cena de Acción de Gracias

EL JARDÍN/EL PATIO (THE GARDEN/THE BACKYARD)

1) **jardinero** (gardener)
hahr-dee-NEH-roh

2) **cobertizo** (shed)
koh-behr-TEE-soh

3) **arbusto** (bush)
ahr-BOOS-toh

4) **césped/grama** (lawn)
SEHS-pehd/GRAH-mah

5) **pasto** (grass)
PAHS-toh

6) **flor** (flower)
flohr

7) **manguera de jardín** (garden hose)
mahn-GEH-rah deh hahr-DEEN

8) **regadera** (watering can)
rreh-gah-DEH-rah

9) **maceta** (flowerpot)
mah-SEH-tah

10) **guantes de jardinería** (gardening
gloves)
GWAHN-tehs deh hahr-dee-neh-REE-
ah

11) **pala** (shovel)
PAH-lah

12) **rastrillo** (rake)
rrahs-TREE-yoh

13) **tenedor de jardinería** (gardening fork)
teh-neh-DOHR deh hahr-dee-neh-
REE-ah

14) **tijeras de podar** (pruners/pruning
shears)
tee-HEH-rahs deh poh-DAHR

15) **paleta de jardín** (garden trowel)
pah-LEH-tah deh hahr-DEEN

16) **grifo** (tap)
GREE-foh

17) **carretilla** (wheelbarrow)
kah-rreh-TEE-yah

18) **podadora de césped** (lawn mower)
poh-dah-DOH-rah deh SEHS-pehd

19) **farol** (lantern)
fah-ROHL

20) **enredadera** (vine)
ehn-rreh-dah-DEH-rah

El jardinero cortó el pasto con una podadora de césped, y luego usó un rastrillo y una carretilla para llevarse todo.
The gardener cut the grass with a lawn mower, and then used a rake and a wheelbarrow to take everything away.

Usa una manguera de jardín para los arbustos, pero una regadera para las flores.
Use a garden hose for the bushes, but a watering can for the flowers.

EL CUARTO DE LIMPIEZA (THE CLEANING ROOM)

1) **lavadora** (washing machine)
lah-vah-DOH-rah

2) **secadora** (dryer)
seh-kah-DOH-rah

3) **plancha** (iron)
PLAHN-chah

4) **tabla de planchar/mesa de planchar**
(ironing board)
TAH-blah/MEH-sah deh plahn-
CHAHR

5) **jabón de lavandería** (laundry soap)
hah-BOHN deh lah-vahn-deh-REE-ah

6) **detergente de lavandería** (laundry
detergent)
deh-tehr-HEHN-teh deh lah-vahn-
deh-REE-ah

7) **suavizante para ropa** (fabric softener)
swah-vee-SAHN-teh PAH-rah RROH-
pah

8) **cesto para ropa** (laundry basket)
SEHS-toh PAH-rah RROH-pah

9) **ropa sucia** (dirty clothes)
RROH-pah SOO-syah

10) **ropa limpia** (clean laundry)
RROH-pah LEEM-pyah

11) **escoba** (broom)
ehs-KOH-bah

12) **recogedor/pala recogedora** (dustpan)
rreh-koh-heh-DOHR/PAH-lah rreh-
koh-heh-DOH-rah

13) **guantes de goma/guantes de caucho**
(rubber gloves)
GWAHN-tehs deh GO-
mah/GWAHN-tehs deh KOW-choh

14) **esponja** (sponge)
ehs-POHN-hah

15) **recipiente de plástico** (plastic tub)
rreh-see-PYEHN-teh deh PLAHS-tee-
koh

16) **fregona/trapeador** (mop)
freh-GOH-nah/trah-peh-ah-DOHR

17) **balde/cubeta** (bucket)
BAHL-deh/koo-BEH-tah

18) **paño de limpieza/trapo de limpieza**
(cleaning cloths)
PAH-nyoh/TRAH-poh deh leem-
PYEH-sah

19) **cepillo para fregar** (scrub brush)
seh-PEE-yoh PAH-rah freh-GAHR

20) **blanqueador/lejía** (bleach)
blahn-keh-ah-DOHR/leh-HEE-ah

21) **desinfectante** (disinfectant)
dehs-een-fehk-TAHN-teh

22) **bote de basura** (garbage can)
BOH-teh deh bah-SOO-rah

*Ella le compró a su hijo detergente de lavandería, suavizante para ropa y un cesto para ropa
para lavar su ropa sucia.*
She bought her son laundry detergent, fabric softener, and a laundry basket to wash his dirty
clothes.

LA ESCUELA/LA UNIVERSIDAD (THE SCHOOL/THE UNIVERSITY)

1) **maestro** (teacher)
mah-EHS-troh

2) **estudiante** (student)
ehs-too-DYAHN-teh

3) **aula/salón de clases** (classroom)
OW-lah/sah-LOHN deh KLAH-sehs

4) **casillero** (locker)
kah-see-YEH-roh

5) **cartelera informativa** (bulletin board)
kahr-teh-LEH-rah een-fohr-mah-TEE-vah

6) **hoja de papel** (sheet of paper)
OH-hah deh pah-PEHL

7) **libro** (book)
LEE-broh

8) **cuaderno** (notebook)
kwah-DEHR-noh

9) **pegamento/pega** (glue)
peh-gah-MEHN-toh/PEH-gah

10) **tijeras** (scissors)
tee-HEH-rahs

11) **lápiz** (pencil)
LAH-pees

12) **borrador** (eraser)
boh-rrah-DOHR

13) **sacapuntas** (pencil sharpener)
sah-kah-POON-tahs

14) **bolígrafo/pluma/lapicera** (pen)
boh-LEE-grah-foh/PLOO-mah/lah-pee-SEH-rah

15) **marcador/rotulador** (marker)
mahr-kah-DOHR/rroh-too-lah-DOHR

16) **marcador fluorescente/resaltador** (highlighter)
mahr-kah-DOHR floo-oh-rehs-SEHN-teh/rreh-sahl-tah-DOHR

17) **sobre** (envelope)
SOH-breh

18) **portapapeles** (clipboard)
pohr-tah-pah-PEH-lehs

19) **pizarra/pizarrón** (blackboard)
pee-SAH-rrah/pee-sah-RROHN

20) **calculadora** (calculator)
kahl-koo-lah-DOH-rah

21) **regla** (ruler)
RREH-glah

22) **grapadora** (stapler)
grah-pah-DOH-rah

23) **cartuchera/caja de lápices** (pouch/pencil case)
kahr-too-CHEH-rah/KAH-hah deh LAH-pee-sehs

24) **pupitre** (school desk)
poo-PEE-treh

25) **mesa** (table)
MEH-sah

26) **computadora portátil/ordenador portátil** (laptop)
kohm-poo-tah-DOH-rah/ohr-deh-nah-DOHR pohr-TAH-teel

En vez de pupitres, los estudiantes están sentados frente a las mesas del aula de clases.
Instead of desks, the students are sitting in front of the tables in the classroom.

El maestro permitió el uso de calculadoras y reglas en el examen.
The teacher allowed the use of calculators and rulers on the test.

LA OFICINA (THE OFFICE)

1) **jefe** (boss)
HEH-feh

2) **superior** (superior)
soo-peh-RYOHR

3) **empleado** (employee)
ehm-pleh-AH-doh

4) **presidente** (CEO/president)
preh-see-DEHN-teh

5) **socio** (business partner)
SOH-syoh

6) **colega** (colleague)
koh-LEH-gah

7) **compañero de trabajo** (co-worker)
kohm-pah-NYEH-roh deh trah-BAH-hoh

8) **secretaria** (secretary)
seh-kreh-TAH-ryah

9) **cubículo** (cubicle)
koo-BEE-koo-loh

10) **silla giratoria** (swivel chair)
SEE-yah hee-rah-TOH-ryah

11) **escritorio** (desk)
ehs-kree-TOH-ryoh

12) **computadora/ordenador** (computer)
kohm-poo-tah-DOH-rah/ohr-deh-nah-DOHR

13) **impresora** (printer)
eem-preh-SOH-rah

14) **artículos de oficina** (office supplies)
ahr-TEE-koo-lohs deh oh-fee-SEE-nah

15) **sello de goma** (rubber stamp)
SEH-yoh deh GOH-mah

16) **dispensador de cinta** (tape dispenser)
dees-pehn-sah-DOHR deh SEEN-tah

17) **carpeta/expediente** (folder)
kahr-PEH-tah/ehks-peh-DYEHN-teh

18) **archivador** (filing cabinet)
ahr-chee-vah-DOHR

19) **fax** (fax)
fahks

20) **teléfono** (telephone)
teh-LEH-foh-noh

Tengo un escitorio pequeño y una silla giratoria en mi cubículo.
I have a small desk and a swivel chair in my cubicle.

El jefe dijo que pusiera la carpeta en el archivador.
The boss said to put the folder in the filing cabinet.

Si necesitas sellos de goma, un dispensador de cinta o cualquier otro artículo de oficina, pídeselo a la secretaria.
If you need rubber stamps, a tape dispenser, or any other office supplies, ask the secretary.

PROFESIONES/OFICIOS (PROFESSIONS/OCCUPATIONS)

1) **ingeniero** (engineer)
eem-heh-NYEH-roh

2) **astronauta** (astronaut)
ahs-troh-NOW-tah

3) **piloto** (pilot)
pee-LOH-toh

4) **juez** (judge)
hwes

5) **bombero** (firefighter)
bohm-BEH-roh

6) **oficial de policía** (police officer)
oh-fee-SYAHL deh poh-lee-SEE-ah

7) **chef** (chef)
chehf

8) **director de orquesta** (conductor)
dee-rehk-TOHR deh ohr-KEHS-tah

9) **profesor** (professor)
proh-feh-SOHR

10) **bailarina** (dancer)
bayh-lah-REE-nah

11) **empresario** (businessman)
ehm-preh-SAH-ryoh

12) **entrenador de animales** (animal trainer)
ehn-treh-nah-DOHR

Fui chef hasta los 30 años, pero luego me convertí en profesor de inglés.
I was a chef until I was 30, but then I became and English professor.

La mayoría de los niños quieren ser bomberos, astronautas u oficiales de policía de grandes, pero mi sobrino siempre quiso ser piloto.
Most kids want to be firemen, astronauts, or police officers when they grow up, but my nephew always wanted to be a pilot.

Mi hermano es ingeniero y su esposa (mi cuñada) es entrenadora de animales.
My brother is an engineer, and his wife (my sister-in-law) is an animal trainer.

MEDIOS DE TRANSPORTE (MEANS OF TRANSPORT)

1) **bicicleta** (bike/bicycle)
bee-see-KLEH-tah

2) **motocicleta** (motorcycle/motorbike)
moh-toh-see-KLEH-tah

3) **motonieve** (snowmobile)
moh-toh-NYE-veh

4) **automóvil/auto** (car/automobile)
ow-toh-MOH-veel

5) **autobús** (bus)
ow-toh-BOOS

6) **camión** (truck)
kah-MYOHN

7) **metro/subterráneo** (subway)
MEH-troh

8) **tren** (train)
trehn

9) **moto acuática** (Jet Ski)
MOH-toh ah-KWAH-tee-kah

10) **bote** (boat)
BOH-teh

11) **crucero** (cruise ship)
kroo-SEH-roh

12) **submarino** (submarine)
soob-mah-REE-noh

13) **dirigible** (blimp/Zeppelin)
dee-ree-HEE-bleh

14) **globo aerostático** (hot-air balloon)
GLOH-boh ah-eh-rohs-TAH-tee-koh

15) **avión** (plane/airplane)
ah-BYON

16) **helicóptero** (helicopter/chopper)
eh-lee-KOHP-teh-roh

17) **transbordador espacial** (space shuttle)
trahns-bohr-dah-DOHR ehs-pah-SYAHL

Tomo el autobús y el metro a todos lados porque no tengo auto.
I take the bus and the subway everywhere because I do not have a car.

He estado en muchos aviones, pero nunca he subido a un helicóptero.
I have been on many planes, but I have never ridden a helicopter.

Mi bisabuela nació antes de los primeros aviones y murió después de la llegada de los transbordadores espaciales.
My great-grandmother was born before the first airplanes and died after the arrival of the space shuttles.

PAISAJES (LANDSCAPES)

1) **montaña** (mountain)
   mohn-TAH-nyah

2) **selva tropical** (tropical rainforest)
   SEHL-vah troh-pee-KAHL

3) **desierto** (desert)
   deh-SYEHR-toh

4) **volcán** (volcano)
   vohl-KAHN

5) **acantilado** (cliff)
   ah-kahn-tee-LAH-doh

6) **playa** (beach)
   PLAH-yah

7) **bosque** (forest)
   BOHS-keh

8) **cueva** (cave)
   KWEH-vah

9) **géiser** (geyser)
   HEY-sehr

10) **cascada/cataratas** (waterfall/falls)
    kahs-KAH-dah/kah-tah-RAH-tahs

11) **río** (river)
    REE-oh

12) **ruinas antiguas** (ancient ruins)
    RRWEE-nahs ahn-TEE-gwas

Siempre he preferido la playa y el bosque, pero mi abuelo amaba el desierto.
I have always preferred the beach and the forest, but my grandfather loved the desert.

Mi hermano y mi cuñada han visitado los volcanes de Hawái, los acantilados de Big Sur y los géiseres de Yellowstone.
My brother and sister-in-law have visited the volcanos of Hawaii, the cliffs of Big Sur, and the geysers of Yellowstone.

Las cuevas y las ruinas antiguas suelen guardar secretos.
Caves and ancient ruins often hold secrets.

DEPORTES I (SPORTS I)

1) **tiro con arco** (archery)
   TEE-roh kohn AHR-koh

2) **boxeo** (boxing)
   bohk-SEH-oh

3) **ciclismo** (cycling)
   see-KLEES-moh

4) **esgrima** (fencing)
   ehs-GREE-mah

5) **fútbol** (football/soccer)
   FOOT-bohl

6) **rugby** (rugby)
   RROOG-bee

7) **tenis de mesa** (table tennis/ping-pong)
   TEH-nees deh MEH-sah

8) **voleibol** (volleyball)
   VOH-ley-bohl

9) **halterofilia** (weightlift)
   ahl-teh-roh-FEE-lyah

10) **patinaje** (skating)
    pah-tee-NAH-heh

11) **deportes paralímpicos** (paralympic sports)
    deh-POHR-tehs pah-rah-LEEM-pee-kohs

12) **béisbol** (baseball)
    BEYS-bohl

13) **baloncesto** (basketball)
    bah-lohn-SEHS-toh

Mi papá jugaba al béisbol, mi hermano jugaba al fútbol y mi sobrino practica tiro con arco, pero a mí nunca me han gustado los deportes.
My father played baseball, my brother played football, and my nephew practices archery, but I have never liked sports.

Juegan al baloncesto en días soleados y tenis de mesa cuando llueve.
They play basketball on sunny days and table tennis when it rains.

DEPORTES II (SPORTS II)

1) **bádminton** (badminton)
BAHD-meen-tohn

2) **gimnasia** (gymnastics)
heem-NAH-syah

3) **remo** (rowing)
RREH-moh

4) **escalada deportiva** (sport climbing)
ehs-kah-LAH-dah deh-pohr-TEE-vah

5) **surf** (surfing)
soorf

6) **tenis** (tennis)
TEH-nees

7) **trampolín** (trampoline)
trahm-poh-LEEN

8) **lucha** (wrestling)
LOO-chah

9) **esquí** (skiing)
ehs-KEE

10) **skeleton/trineo simple** (skeleton)
ehs-KEH-leh-tohn/tree-NEH-oh
SEEM-pleh

11) **patinaje artístico** (figure skating)
pah-tee-NAH-heh ahr-TEES-tee-koh

12) **natación** (swimming)
nah-tah-SYOHN

13) **waterpolo** (water polo)
wah-tehr-POH-loh

14) **hockey** (hockey)
HOH-kee

La natación es uno de los mejores deportes para la salud general.
Swimming is one of the best sports for overall health.

A su exesposo le gustaba el esquí sobre nieve y a su familia el esquí en agua, pero ella solo quería jugar al tenis.
Her ex-husband liked snow skiing and her family enjoyed water skiing, but she only wanted to play tennis.

EL DÍA DE NAVIDAD (CHRISTMAS DAY)

1) **muérdago** (mistletoe)
MWEHR-dah-goh

2) **guirnalda** (garland)
geer-NAHL-dah

3) **árbol de Navidad** (Christmas tree)
AHR-bohl deh nah-vee-DAHD

4) **decoraciones navideñas/adornos de Navidad** (Christmas decorations)
deh-koh-rah-SYO-nehs nah-vee-DEH-nyahs/ah-DOHR-nohs deh nah-vee-DAHD

5) **regalos/presentes de Navidad** (Christmas gifts/presents)
rreh-GAH-lohs/preh-SEHN-tehs deh nah-vee-DAHD

6) **cena de Navidad** (Christmas dinner)
SEH-nah deh nah-vee-DAHD

7) **bastón de caramelo** (candy cane)
bahs-TOHN deh kah-rah-MEH-loh

8) **hombre de jengibre** (gingerbread man)
OHM-breh deh hehn-HEE-breh

9) **elfo de Navidad** (Christmas elf)
EHL-foh deh nah-vee-DAHD

10) **gorro de Navidad** (Christmas hat)
GOH-rroh de nah-vee-DAHD

11) **Santa Claus/Papá Noel** (Santa Claus)
SAHN-tah klows/pah-PAH noh-EHL

12) **trineo de Santa** (Santa's sleigh)
tree-NEH-oh deh SAHN-tah

13) **estrella de Navidad** (Christmas star)
ehs-TREH-yah deh nah-vee-DAHD

14) **muñeco de nieve/hombre de nieve** (snowman)
moo-NYEH-koh deh NYEH-veh/OHM-breh de NYEH-veh

15) **velas** (candles)
VEH-lahs

No ponemos decoraciones navideñas en nuestra casa, ya que mis suegros tienen un árbol de Navidad y celebramos la cena de Navidad allí.
We do not put Christmas decorations up in our house, as my parents-in-law have a Christmas tree and we celebrate Christmas dinner there.

Mi hija comió demasiados bastones de caramelo y hombres de jengibre la Navidad pasada.
My daughter ate too many candy canes and gingerbread men last Christmas.

Ella les dijo a los niños que se pusieran sus gorros navideños antes de salir a hacer un hombre de nieve.
She told the children to put on their Christmas hats before going out to make a snowman.

QUIZ #4

Use arrows to match the corresponding translations:

a. cruise ship

b. firefighter

c. washing machine

d. Christmas tree

e. river

f. shed

g. wrestling

h. teacher

i. dirty clothes

j. employee

k. basketball

l. train

m. desert

n. shovel

o. snowman

p. scissors

1. lucha

2. empleado

3. río

4. tren

5. crucero

6. baloncesto

7. lavadora

8. muñeco de nieve/hombre de nieve

9. maestro

10. bombero

11. pala

12. cobertizo

13. tijeras

14. árbol de Navidad

15. desierto

16. ropa sucia

Fill in the blank spaces with the options below (use each word only once):

Martha es una _____ universitaria que quiere ser _____. En sus ratos libres ama estar al aire libre, ir a la _____ a practicar _____ y también practicar _____, yendo a todos lados en su _____. En diciembre se atravesó un perro en su camino, entonces ella se lanzó hacia un _____ para no lastimarlo y ensució su traje de _____. Por suerte, el _____ fue suficiente para quitar el sucio, y la _____ hizo el resto del trabajo. Si su _____ lo nota, seguramente no le gustará… aunque no le dirá nada ¡porque él es _____!

elfo de Navidad	bicicleta
secadora	surf
jefe	Santa Claus / Papá Noel
detergente de lavandería	arbusto
playa	estudiante
ingeniera	ciclismo

INSTRUMENTOS MUSICALES (MUSICAL INSTRUMENTS)

1) **guitarra acústica** (acoustic guitar)
gee-TAH-rrah ah-KOOS-tee-kah

2) **guitarra eléctrica** (electric guitar)
gee-TAH-rrah eh-LEHK-tree-kah

3) **bajo** (bass guitar)
BAH-hoh

4) **batería** (drums)
bah-teh-REE-ah

5) **piano** (piano)
PYAH-noh

6) **trompeta** (trumpet)
trohm-PEH-tah

7) **armónica** (harmonica)
ahr-MOH-nee-kah

8) **flauta** (flute)
FLOW-tah

9) **clarinete** (clarinet)
klah-ree-NEH-teh

10) **arpa** (harp)
AHR-pah

11) **gaita** (bagpipes)
GAYH-tah

12) **violonchelo** (cello)
vyoh-lohn-CHEH-loh

13) **violín** (violin)
vyoh-LEEN

14) **saxofón** (saxophone)
sahk-soh-FOHN

Yo tocaba el clarinete en la escuela primaria, y mi mejor amigo tocaba la flauta.
I played the clarinet in elementary school and my best friend played the flute.

Mike siempre fue un genio con la guitarra eléctrica, pero se cambió a la batería hace varios años.
Mike was always a genius on the electric guitar, but he switched to drums several years ago.

Ella quería una gaita, pero solo tuvo el dinero para una armónica.
She wanted bagpipes, but she only had money for a harmonica.

FRUTAS (FRUITS)

1) **fresa** (strawberry)
FREH-sah

2) **papaya** (papaya)
pah-PAH-yah

3) **ciruela** (plum)
see-RWEH-lah

4) **melón** (melon)
meh-LOHN

5) **sandía** (watermelon)
sahn-DEE-ah

6) **banana** (banana)
bah-NAH-nah

7) **mango** (mango)
MAHN-goh

8) **melocotón/durazno** (peach)
meh-loh-koh-TOHN/doo-RAHS-noh

9) **frambuesa** (raspberry)
frahm-BWEH-sah

10) **naranja** (orange)
nah-RAHN-hah

11) **limón** (lemon)
lee-MOHN

12) **piña** (pineapple)
PEE-nya

13) **lima** (lime)
LEE-mah

14) **uvas** (grapes)
OO-vahs

15) **cereza** (cherry)
seh-REH-sah

16) **manzana** (apple)
mahn-SAH-nah

17) **pera** (pear)
PEH-rah

18) **pomelo/toronja** (grapefruit)
poh-MEH-loh/toh-ROHN-hah

19) **guanábana** (soursop)
gwah-NAH-bah-nah

20) **coco** (coconut)
KOH-koh

Prefiero las fresas a las frambuesas por las semillas.
I prefer strawberries to raspberries because of the seeds.

Los limones y las limas son ricos, pero los pomelos no.
Lemons and limes are delicious, but grapefruits are not.

Hice pasteles de cereza, de manzana y de durazno.
I made cherry, apple, and peach pies.

VEGETALES (VEGETABLES)

1) **coliflor** (cauliflower)
koh-lee-FLOHR

2) **espárragos** (asparagus)
ehs-PAH-rrah-gohs

3) **brócoli** (broccoli)
BROH-koh-lee

4) **repollo/col** (cabbage)
rreh-POH-yoh/kohl

5) **alcachofa** (artichoke)
ahl-kah-CHOH-fah

6) **coles de Bruselas** (Brussels sprouts)
KOH-lehs deh broo-SEH-lahs

7) **maíz** (corn)
mah-EES

8) **lechuga** (lettuce)
leh-CHOO-gah

9) **espinaca** (spinach)
ehs-pee-NAH-kah

10) **tomate** (tomato)
toh-MAH-teh

11) **pepino** (cucumber)
peh-PEE-noh

12) **calabacín** (zucchini)
kah-lah-bah-SEEN

13) **hongo/champiñón/seta** (mushroom)
OHN-goh/chahm-pee-NYON/SEH-tah

14) **rúcula/arúgula** (arugula)
ROO-koo-lah/ah-ROO-goo-lah

15) **berenjena** (eggplant)
beh-rehn-HEH-nah

16) **pimentón/pimiento morrón** (bell pepper)
pee-mehn-TOHN/pee-MYEHN-toh moh-RROHN

17) **cebolla** (onion)
seh-BOH-yah

18) **calabaza** (pumpkin)
kah-lah-BAH-sah

19) **papa/patata** (potato)
PAH-pah/pah-TAH-tah

20) **acelga** (Swiss chard)
ah-SEHL-gah

Las coles de Bruselas, la coliflor, el brócoli y el repollo son de la misma familia de vegetales.
Brussels sprouts, cauliflower, broccoli, and cabbage are from the same family of vegetables.

Vegetales verdes como la rúcula, espinaca y acelga son ricos en hierro.
Green vegetables like arugula, spinach, and Swiss chard are rich in iron.

El maíz es un alimento básico en Centroamérica.
Corn is a staple food in Central America.

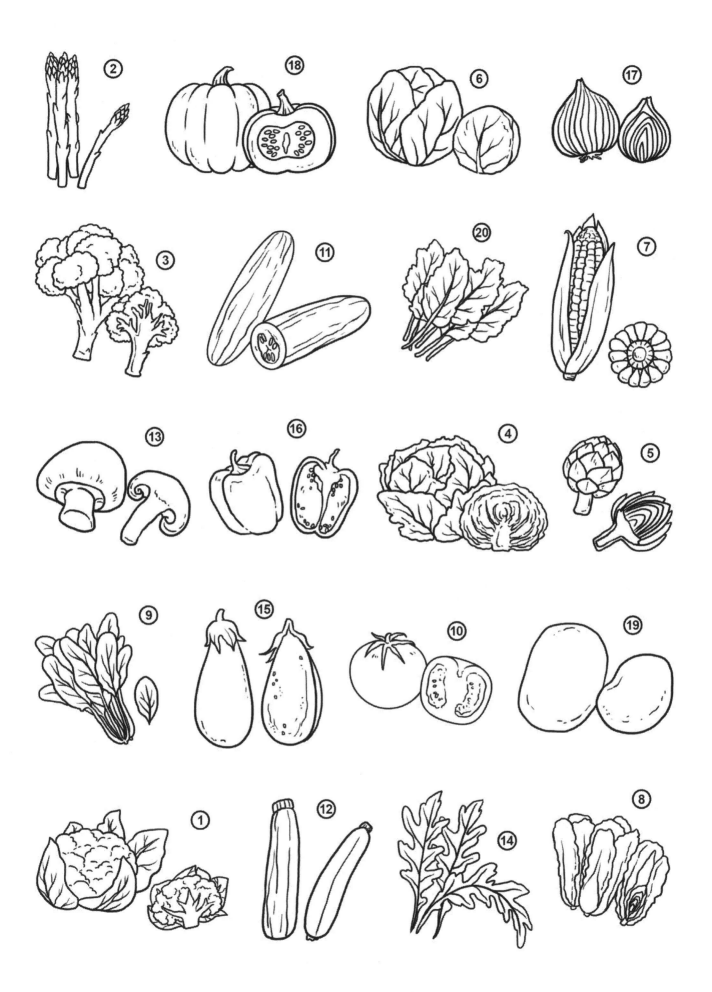

TECNOLOGÍA (TECHNOLOGY)

1) **móvil** (mobile)
   MOH-veel

2) **dispositivo** (device)
   dees-poh-see-TEE-voh

3) **computadora** (computer)
   kohm-poo-tah-DOH-rah

4) **cámara web** (web cam)
   KAH-mah-rah web

5) **unidad flash/memoria flash/pendrive** (flash drive)
   oo-nee-DAHD flash/meh-MOH-ryah flash/PEHN-drayv

6) **disco duro** (hard drive)
   DEES-koh DOO-roh

7) **tarjeta de memoria** (memory card)
   tahr-HEH-tah deh meh-MOH-ryah

8) **lector de tarjetas** (card reader)
   lehk-TOHR deh tahr-HEH-tahs

9) **inalámbrico** (wireless)
   ee-nah-LAHM-bree-koh

10) **panel solar** (solar panel)
    pah-NEHL soh-LAHR

11) **impresora** (printer)
    eem-preh-SOH-rah

12) **escáner** (scanner)
    ehs-KAH-nehr

Este dispositivo es una impresora y escáner inalámbrico.
This device is a wireless scanner and printer.

El virus en la memoria flash dañó el disco duro de mi computadora.
The virus on the flash drive damaged the hard drive on my computer.

CIENCIA (SCIENCE)

1) **laboratorio** (laboratory)
   lah-boh-rah-TOH-ryoh

2) **investigador** (researcher)
   een-vehs-tee-gah-DOHR

3) **cálculos** (calculations)
   KAHL-koo-lohs

4) **científico** (scientist)
   syehn-TEE-fee-koh

5) **bata de laboratorio** (lab coat)
   BAH-tah deh lah-boh-rah-TOH-ryoh

6) **experimento** (experiment)
   eks-peh-ree-MEHN-toh

7) **equipo de protección personal** (personal protective equipment)
   eh-KEE-poh deh proh-tehk-SYOHN pehr-soh-NAHL

8) **prueba** (test)
   PRWEH-bah

9) **premio** (prize)
   PREH-myoh

10) **riesgo** (risk)
    RRYEHS-goh

11) **instrumento** (instrument)
    eens-troo-MEHN-toh

12) **estadística** (statistics)
    ehs-tah-DEES-tee-kah

El investigador hace los cálculos para llevar a cabo el experimento en el laboratorio.
The researcher does the calculations to carry out the experiment in the laboratory.

La científica usa equipo de protección personal para reducir el riesgo durante la prueba.
The scientist uses personal protective equipment to reduce the risk during the test.

Él guarda sus instrumentos en su bata de laboratorio.
He keeps his instruments in his lab coat.

ASTRONOMÍA (ASTRONOMY)

1) **telescopio** (telescope)
teh-lehs-KOH-pyoh

2) **sol** (sun)
sohl

3) **luna** (moon)
LOO-nah

4) **galaxia** (galaxy)
gah-LAHK-syah

5) **cinturón de asteroides** (asteroid belt)
seen-too-ROHN deh ahs-teh-ROY-
dehs

6) **agujero negro** (black hole)
ah-goo-HEH-roh NEH-groh

7) **eclipse** (eclipse)
eh-KLEEP-seh

8) **estrella fugaz** (shooting star)
ehs-TREH-yah foo-GAHS

9) **estación espacial** (space station)
ehs-tah-SYOHN ehs-pah-SYAHL

10) **enana blanca** (white dwarf)
eh-NAH-nah BLAHN-kah

11) **gigante roja** (red giant)
hee-GAHN-teh RROH-hah

12) **órbita** (orbit)
OHR-bee-tah

13) **constelación** (constellation)
kohns-teh-lah-SYOHN

14) **energía oscura** (dark energy)
eh-nehr-HEE-ah ohs-KOO-rah

15) **Plutón** (Pluto)
ploo-TOHN

16) **Nebulosa** (Nebula)
neh-boo-LOH-sah

17) **Mercurio** (Mercury)
mehr-KOO-ryoh

18) **Venus** (Venus)
VEH-noos

19) **Tierra** (Earth)
TYEH-rrah

20) **Marte** (Mars)
MAHR-teh

21) **Júpiter** (Jupiter)
HOO-pee-tehr

22) **Saturno** (Saturn)
sah-TOOR-noh

23) **Urano** (Uranus)
oo-RAH-noh

24) **Neptuno** (Neptune)
nehp-TOO-noh

La estación espacial está en una órbita de 90 minutos alrededor de la Tierra.
The space station is in a 90-minute orbit around the Earth.

Vimos estrellas fugaces anoche mientras mirábamos las constelaciones a través de nuestro telescopio.
We saw shooting stars last night while looking at the constellations through our telescope.

Cuando yo era niño, Plutón aún era un planeta.
When I was a child, Pluto was still a planet.

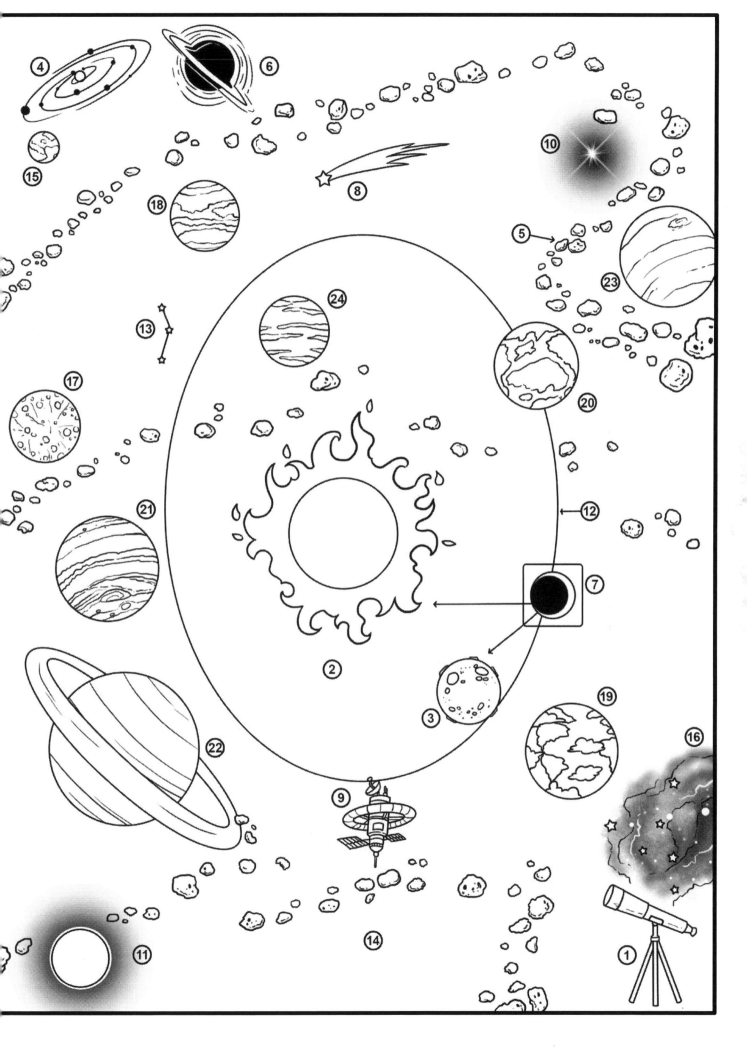

GEOGRAFÍA (GEOGRAPHY)

1) **norte** (north)
NOHR-teh

2) **este** (east)
EHS-teh

3) **sur** (south)
soor

4) **oeste** (west)
oh-EHS-teh

5) **Ecuador** (Equator)
eh-kwah-DOHR

6) **Trópico de Cáncer** (Tropic of Cancer)
TROH-pee-koh deh KAHN-sehr

7) **Trópico de Capricornio** (Tropic of Capricorn)
TROH-pee-koh deh kah-pree-KOHR-nyoh

8) **Polo Sur** (South Pole)
POH-loh SOOR

9) **Polo Norte** (North Pole)
POH-loh NOHR-teh

10) **Círculo Polar Ártico** (Arctic Circle)
SEER-koo-loh poh-LAHR AHR-tee-koh

11) **continente** (continent)
kohn-tee-NEHN-teh

12) **de ultramar** (overseas)
deh ool-trah-MAHR

13) **África** (Africa)
AH-free-kah

14) **Asia** (Asia)
AH-syah

15) **Norteamérica** (North America)
nohr-teh-ah-MEH-ree-kah

16) **Centroamérica** (Central America)
sehn-troh-ah-MEH-ree-kah

17) **Suramérica** (South America)
soo-rah-MEH-ree-kah

18) **Europa** (Europe)
ehoo-ROH-pah

19) **Oceanía** (Oceania)
oh-seh-ah-NEE-ah

20) **Antártida** (Antarctica)
ahn-TAHR-tee-dah

21) **meridiano** (meridian)
meh-ree-DYAH-noh

22) **paralelo** (parallel)
pah-rah-LEH-loh

23) **Océano Atlántico** (Atlantic Ocean)
oh-SEH-ah-noh ah-TLAHN-tee-koh

24) **Océano Pacífico** (Pacific Ocean)
oh-SEH-ah-noh pah-SEE-fee-koh

Todos en mi familia son del oeste, excepto mi abuela, quien es del sur.
Everyone in my family is from the west, except for my grandmother, who is from the south.

En la escuela aprendí que había siete continentes, pero Norteamérica y Suramérica se cuentan como uno en muchas partes del mundo.
I learned in school that there were seven continents, but North America and South America are counted as one in many parts of the world.

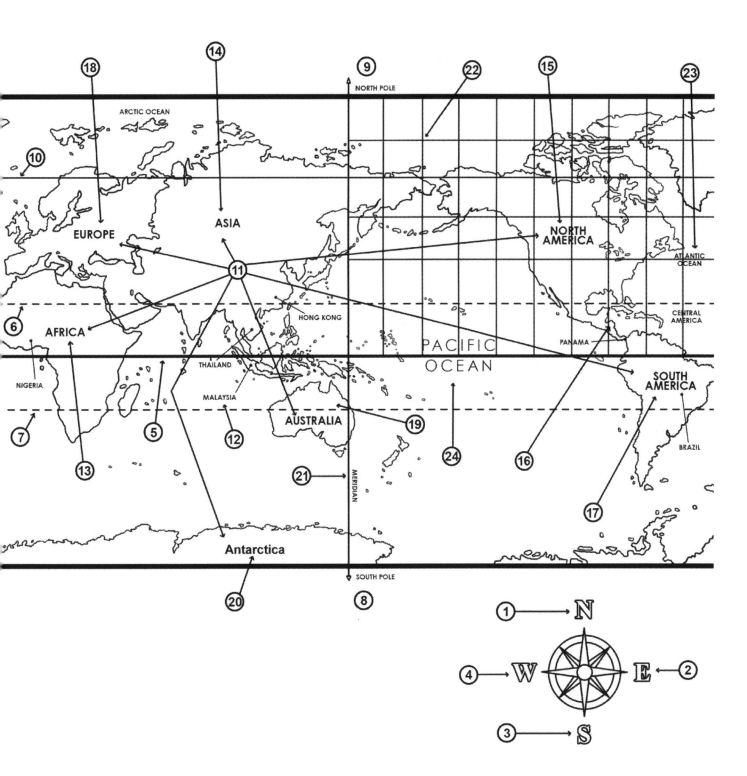

EL HOSPITAL (THE HOSPITAL)

1) **doctor/médico** (doctor/medic)
dohk-TOHR/MEH-dee-koh

2) **enfermera** (nurse)
ehn-fehr-MEH-rah

3) **ambulancia** (ambulance)
ahm-boo-LAHN-syah

4) **botiquín de primeros auxilios** (first-aid kit)
boh-tee-KEEN deh pree-MEH-rohs owk-SEE-lyohs

5) **termómetro** (thermometer)
tehr-MOH-meh-troh

6) **camilla** (stretcher)
kah-MEE-yah

7) **jeringa** (syringe)
heh-REEN-gah

8) **aguja** (needle)
ah-GOO-hah

9) **estetoscopio** (stethoscope)
ehs-teh-tohs-KOH-pyoh

10) **muletas** (crutches)
moo-LEH-tahs

11) **silla de ruedas** (wheelchair)
SEE-yah deh RRWEH-dahs

12) **sala de observación** (observation room)
SAH-lah deh ohb-sehr-vah-SYOHN

13) **cama de hospital** (hospital bed)
KAH-mah deh ohs-pee-TAHL

14) **inyección** (injection)
een-yehk-SYOHN

15) **cirugía** (surgery)
see-roo-HEE-ah

16) **historia clínica** (medical history)
ees-TOH-ryah KLEE-nee-kah

17) **paciente** (patient)
pah-SYEHN-teh

18) **píldora/pastilla** (pill/tablet)
PEEL-doh-rah/pahs-TEE-yah

Tú ve por el botiquín de primeros auxilios y yo llamaré a una ambulancia.
You get the first-aid kit and I will call an ambulance.

Después de mi cirugía en la cadera, usé muletas por un mes, pero nunca necesité una silla de ruedas.
After my hip surgery, I used crutches for a month, but I never needed a wheelchair.

Necesitará una inyección en vez de una pastilla; por favor, tráeme una jeringa.
She will need an injection instead of a pill; please, bring me a syringe.

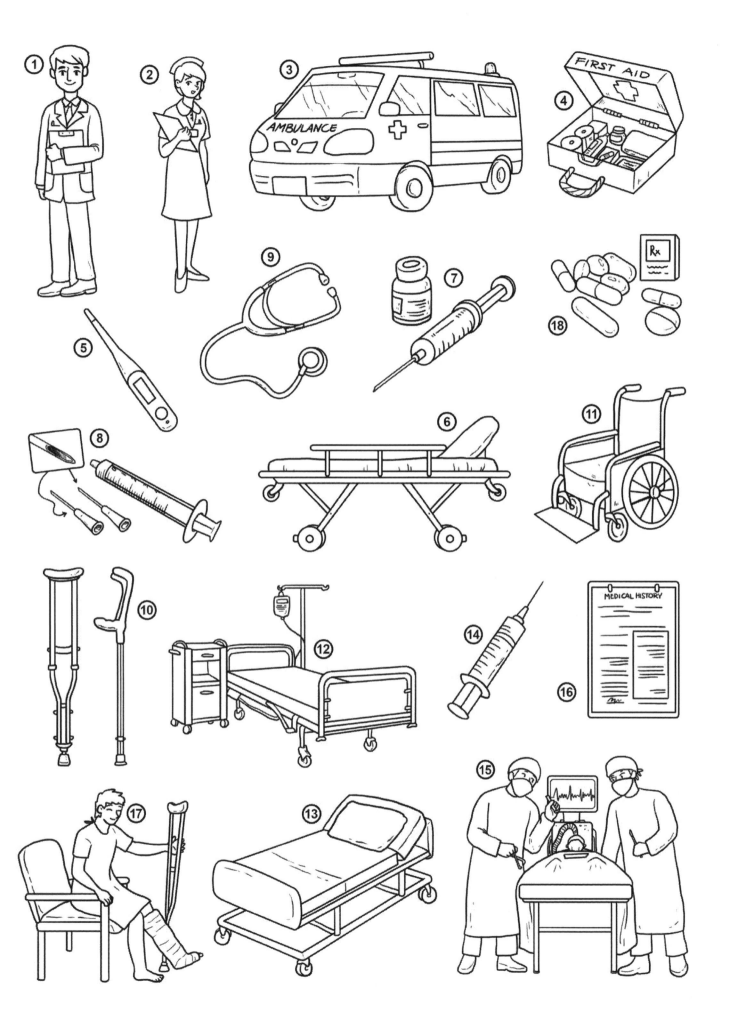

LA GRANJA (THE FARM)

1) **granero** (barn)
grah-NEH-roh

2) **establo** (cowshed/stable)
ehs-TAH-bloh

3) **granjero** (farmer)
grahn-HEH-roh

4) **arado** (plough)
ah-RAH-do

5) **silo** (silo)
SEE-loh

6) **molino** (mill)
moh-LEE-noh

7) **abrevadero** (water trough)
ah-breh-vah-DEH-roh

8) **gallinero** (henhouse)
gah-yee-NEH-roh

9) **colmena/avispero** (beehive)
kohl-MEH-nah/ah-vees-PEH-roh

10) **fardo de heno** (hay bale)
FAHR-doh deh EH-noh

11) **ganado** (cattle)
gah-NAH-doh

12) **ordeñar** (to milk)
ohr-deh-NYAHR

13) **rebaño** (herd/flock)
rreh-BAH-nyoh

14) **gallina** (hen)
gah-YEE-nah

15) **pozo** (well)
POH-soh

16) **sistema de riego** (irrigation system)
sees-TEH-mah deh RRYEH-goh

17) **espantapájaros** (scarecrow)
ehs-pahn-tah-PAH-hah-rohs

18) **camino de tierra** (dirt road)
kah-MEE-noh deh TYEH-rrah

El granjero conectó un sistema de riego a su pozo.
The farmer connected an irrigation system to his well.

Pasamos dos espantapájaros en el camino de tierra hacia el granero.
We passed two scarecrows on the dirt road to the barn.

El ganado vive en el establo, mientras que las gallinas viven en el gallinero.
The cattle live in the stable, while the hens live in the henhouse.

QUIZ #5

Use arrows to match the corresponding translations:

a. apple

b. sun

c. Pacific Ocean

d. printer

e. dirt road

f. cucumber

g. scientist

h. needle

i. pineapple

j. acoustic guitar

k. drums

l. test

m. south

n. hen

o. telescope

p. artichoke

1. batería

2. camino de tierra

3. guitarra acústica

4. aguja

5. telescopio

6. manzana

7. gallina

8. océano Pacífico

9. sur

10. pepino

11. alcachofa

12. impresora

13. sol

14. prueba

15. piña

16. científico

Fill in the blank spaces with the options below (use each word only once):

Lucas trabaja como _____ para un observatorio astronómico en un pueblo al _____ de _____. Cuando era niño vivía en una granja, cuidando el _____ y ayudando a sus padres a sembrar _____ y _____, entre otras cosas. En las noches le gustaba ver la _____, pero también miraba el cielo esperando que pasara una _____ mientras su madre tocaba la _____. Allí se enamoró de la astronomía. Una noche se encontró sin querer con una _____, y las avispas salieron furiosas a atacarlo mientras él corría hacia la casa. Sus padres lo llevaron al hospital de inmediato, pues era alérgico a las picaduras de insectos, y lo atendió una _____ muy amable. Con un _____ muy curioso le inyectó epinefrina, y todos se sintieron muy aliviados de que solo fue un susto.

maíz	investigador
estrella fugaz	armónica
ganado	dispositivo
enfermera	Asia
luna	colmena
este	sandías

COMIDA/ALIMENTOS (FOOD)

1) **pasa** (raisin)
PAH-sah

2) **frutos secos** (nuts)
FROO-tohs SEH-kohs

3) **carne** (meat)
KAHR-neh

4) **cordero** (lamb)
kohr-DEH-roh

5) **pescado** (fish)
pehs-KAH-doh

6) **pollo** (chicken)
POH-yoh

7) **pavo** (turkey)
PAH-voh

8) **miel** (honey)
mee-EHL

9) **azúcar** (sugar)
ah-SOO-kahr

10) **sal** (salt)
sahl

11) **pimienta** (pepper)
pee-MYEHN-tah

12) **tocino/tocineta** (bacon)
toh-SEE-noh/toh-see-NEH-tah

13) **salchichas** (sausages)
sahl-CHEE-chahs

14) **salsa de tomate** (ketchup)
SAHL-sah deh toh-MAH-teh

15) **mayonesa** (mayonnaise)
mah-yoh-NEH-sah

16) **mostaza** (mustard)
mohs-TAH-sah

17) **mermelada** (jam)
mehr-meh-LAH-dah

18) **mantequilla** (butter)
mahn-teh-KEE-yah

19) **jugo** (juice)
HOO-goh

20) **leche** (milk)
LEH-cheh

A ella le gustan todos los frutos secos excepto las almendras.
She likes all nuts except for almonds.

Siempre comíamos jamón en la comida navideña, pero mis primos griegos comían cordero.
We always ate ham for Christmas dinner, but my Greek cousins ate lamb.

Me gusta mucha mostaza y poca mayonesa en mis emparedados de pavo.
I like a lot of mustard and a little mayonnaise on my turkey sandwiches.

PLATOS (DISHES)

1) **lasaña** (lasagna)
   lah-SAH-nyah

2) **tortilla de patatas** (potato omelette)
   tohr-TEE-yah deh pah-TAH-tahs

3) **pastel de carne** (meatloaf)
   pahs-TEHL deh KAHR-neh

4) **fideos fritos** (fried noodles)
   fee-DEH-ohs FREE-tohs

5) **macarrones con queso** (macaroni and cheese)
   mah-kah-RROH-nehs kohn KEH-soh

6) **paella** (paella)
   pah-EH-yah

7) **costillas a la barbacoa** (barbecue ribs)
   kohs-TEE-yahs ah lah bahr-bah-KOH-ah

8) **pan de maíz** (cornbread)
   pahn deh mah-EES

9) **rollo de primavera** (spring roll)
   RROH-yoh deh pree-mah-VEH-rah

10) **hamburguesa con queso** (cheeseburger)
    ahm-boor-GEH-sah kohn KEH-soh

11) **pollo frito** (fried chicken)
    POH-yoh FREE-toh

12) **ensalada César** (Caesar salad)
    ehn-sah-LAH-dah SEH-sahr

13) **sopa de cebolla** (onion soup)
    SOH-pah deh seh-BOH-yah

14) **ensalada de col** (coleslaw)
    ehn-sah-LAH-dah deh KOHL

15) **alitas de pollo picantes** (spicy chicken wings)
    ah-LEE-tahs deh POH-yoh pee-KAHN-tehs

16) **galletas con chispas de chocolate** (chocolate-chip cookies)
    gah-YEH-tahs kohn CHEES-pahs deh choh-koh-LAH-teh

17) **pastel de lima/pie de limón** (key lime pie)
    pahs-TEHL deh LEE-mah/payh deh lee-MOHN

18) **tarta de queso** (cheesecake)
    TAHR-tah deh KEH-soh

Costillas a la barbacoa, ensalada de col y pan de maíz fue la comida favorita de mi abuela en el verano.
Barbecue ribs, cole slaw, and cornbread was my grandmother's favorite meal in the summer.

Prefiero galletas con chispas de chocolate que pie de limón.
I prefer chocolate-chip cookies to key lime pie.

Yo quiero la sopa de cebolla, y la dama pedirá la ensalada César.
I want the onion soup and the lady will have the Ceasar salad.

PRODUCTOS DEL MAR (SEAFOOD)

1) **anchoa** (anchovy)
   ahn-CHOH-ah

2) **bacalao** (cod)
   bah-kah-LAH-oh

3) **centolla** (spider crab)
   sehn-TOH-yah

4) **caballa** (mackerel)
   kah-BAH-yah

5) **langosta** (lobster)
   lahn-GOHS-tah

6) **vieira** (scallop)
   BYEYH-rah

7) **pargo** (snapper)
   PAHR-goh

8) **hueva de salmón** (salmon roe)
   WEH-vah deh sahl-MOHN

9) **cangrejo** (crab)
   kahn-GREH-hoh

10) **mariscos** (shellfish)
    mah-REES-kohs

11) **anguila** (eel)
    ahn-GEE-lah

12) **camarón/gamba** (shrimp)
    kah-mah-ROHN/GAHM-bah

Los mariscos son muy populares durante la Cuaresma, mientras que el bacalao tradicionalmente se sirve en Navidad.
Shellfish are very popular during Lent, while cod is traditionally served at Christmas.

No sé que es peor, la piña en la pizza o la anchoa.
I don't know what's worse, pineapple on pizza or anchovy.

FORMAS (SHAPES)

1) **círculo** (circle)
SEER-koo-loh

2) **óvalo** (oval)
OH-vah-loh

3) **triángulo** (triangle)
tree-AHN-goo-loh

4) **rectángulo** (rectangle)
rehk-TAHN-goo-loh

5) **cuadrado** (square)
kwah-DRAH-doh

6) **trapezoide** (trapezoid)
trah-peh-SOY-deh

7) **rombo** (rhombus)
RROHM-boh

8) **cubo** (cube)
KOO-boh

9) **pentágono** (pentagon)
pehn-TAH-goh-noh

10) **hexágono** (hexagon)
hek-SAH-goh-noh

11) **flecha** (arrow)
FLEH-chah

12) **cruz** (cross)
kroos

13) **corazón** (heart)
koh-rah-SOHN

14) **estrella** (star)
ehs-TREH-yah

15) **cilindro** (cylinder)
see-LEEN-droh

16) **cono** (cone)
KOH-noh

17) **pirámide** (pyramid)
pee-RAH-mee-deh

18) **esfera** (sphere)
ehs-FEH-rah

19) **prisma** (prism)
PREES-mah

Él lleva una cruz alrededor de su cuello, mientras que ella lleva un corazón.
He wears a cross around his neck, while she wears a heart.

Reprobaron el examen porque no sabían la diferencia entre un trapezoide y un rombo.
They failed the test because they didn't know the difference between a trapezoid and a rhombus.

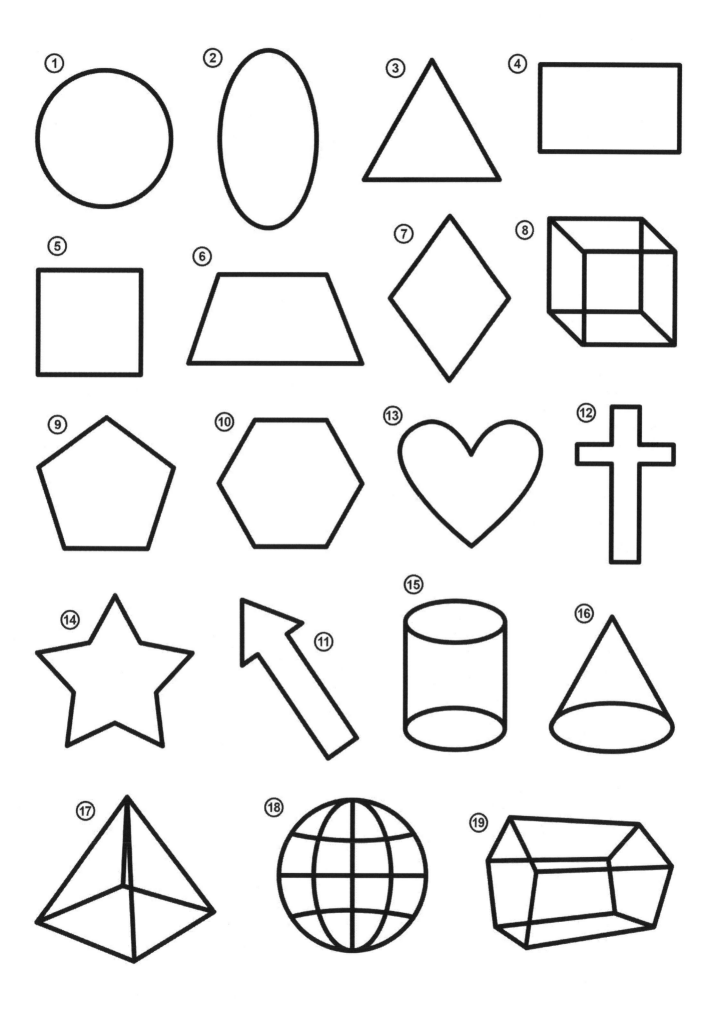

EL SUPERMERCADO (THE SUPERMARKET)

1) **carro de compras** (shopping cart)
KAH-rroh deh KOHM-prahs

2) **vitrina** (cabinet/display case)
vee-TREE-nah

3) **comprador/cliente** (customer)
kohm-prah-DOHR/klee-EHN-teh

4) **cajero** (cashier)
kah-HEH-roh

5) **recibo** (receipt)
rreh-SEE-boh

6) **panadería** (bakery)
pah-nah-deh-REE-ah

7) **frutas y vegetales** (fruits and vegetables)
FROO-tahs y veh-heh-TAH-lehs

8) **carnes** (meat)
KAHR-nehs

9) **productos lácteos** (dairy products)
proh-DOOK-tohs LAHK-teh-ohs

10) **pescados** (fish)
pehs-KAH-dohs

11) **comida congelada/alimentos congelados** (frozen food)
koh-MEE-dah/ah-lee-MEHN-tohs kohn-heh-LAH-dohs

12) **aves** (poultry)
AH-vehs

13) **legumbres** (pulses)
leh-GOOM-brehs

14) **bocadillos** (snacks)
boh-kah-DEE-yohs

15) **postres** (dessert)
POHS-trehs

16) **bebidas** (drinks)
beh-BEE-dahs

17) **artículos del hogar** (household items)
ahr-TEE-koo-lohs dehl oh-GAHR

18) **cinta transportadora/banda transportadora** (belt conveyor)
SEEN-tah/BAHN-dah trahns-pohr-tah-DOH-rah

Yo como muchas frutas y vegetales, algo de pescado y aves, y poca carne.
I eat a lot of fruits and vegetables, some fish and poultry, and little meat.

Al cajero se le olvidó darme mi recibo, así que no puedo devolver los artículos del hogar.
The cashier forgot to give me my receipt, so I cannot return the household items.

Evita bocadillos y bebidas entre comidas.
Avoid snacks and drinks between meals.

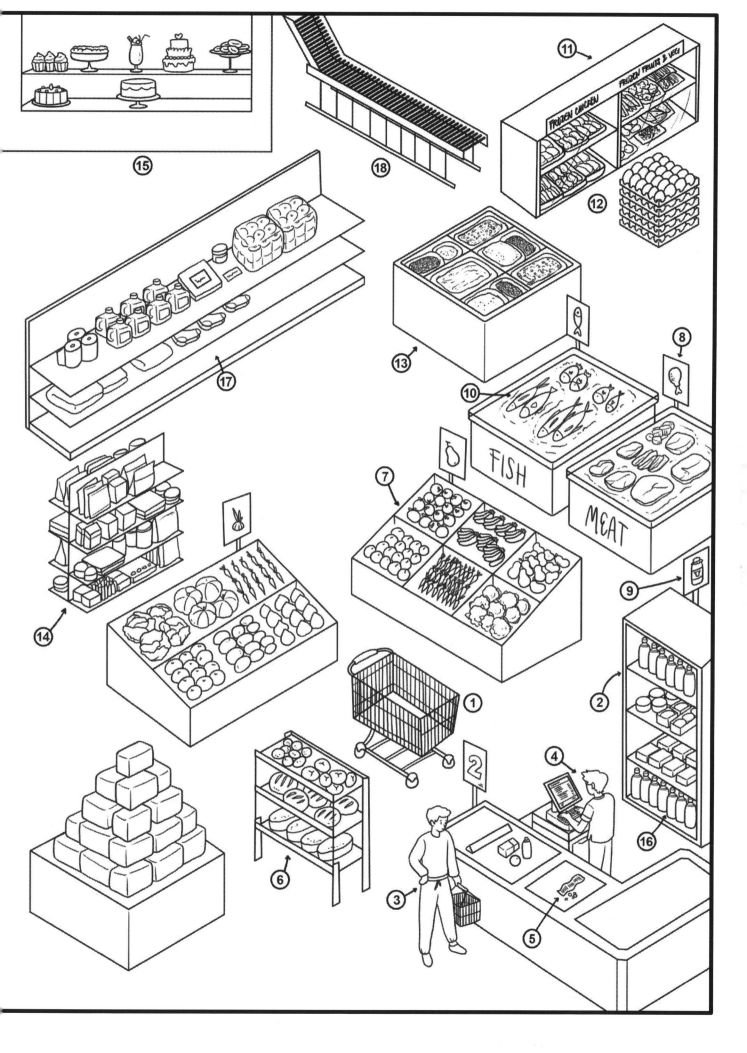

FROZEN CHICKEN
FROZEN FRUITS & VEG

FISH

MEAT

MEDIOS DE COMUNICACIÓN (MEDIA)

1) **revista** (magazine)
rreh-VEES-tah

2) **fax** (fax)
fahks

3) **diario/periódico** (journal)
DYAh-ryoh/peh-ree-OH-dee-koh

4) **correo postal** (postal mail)
koh-RREH-oh pohs-TAHL

5) **carta** (letter)
KAHR-tah

6) **radio** (radio)
RRAH-dyoh

7) **historieta** (comic)
ees-toh-RYEH-tah

8) **libro** (book)
LEE-broh

9) **fotografía** (photography)
foh-toh-grah-FEE-ah

10) **teléfono fijo** (landline phone)
teh-LEH-foh-noh FEE-hoh

11) **televisión** (TV)
teh-leh-vee-SYOHN

12) **cine/películas** (movies)
SEE-neh/peh-LEE-koo-lahs

13) **teléfono móvil/celular** (mobile phone/cellphone)
teh-LEH-foh-noh MOH-veel/seh-loo-LAHR

14) **lenguaje de señas** (sign language)
lehn-GWAH-heh deh SEH-nyahs

El libro siempre es mejor que la película.
The book is always better than the movie.

Por favor, envíame un mensaje, ya que nunca contesto mi teléfono móvil.
Please send me a message, as I never answer my mobile phone.

Ella siempre quiere escuchar la radio cuando él está viendo la televisión.
She always wants to listen to the radio when he is watching TV.

LA FERIA/EL PARQUE DE DIVERSIONES (THE FAIR/THE AMUSEMENT PARK)

1) **laberinto de espejos** (house of mirrors)
lah-beh-REEN-toh deh ehs-PEH-hohs

2) **barco pirata/barco vikingo** (pirate ship/boat swing)
BAHR-koh pee-RAH-tah/BAHR-koh vee-KEEN-goh

3) **taquilla/boletería/oficina de boletos** (ticket booth)
tah-KEE-yah/boh-leh-teh-REE-ah/oh-fee-SEE-nah deh boh-LEH-tohs

4) **sillas voladoras** (swing ride)
SEE-yahs voh-lah-DOH-rahs

5) **montaña rusa** (roller coaster)
mohn-TAH-nyah RROO-sah

6) **noria/rueda de la fortuna** (Ferris wheel)
NOH-ryah/RRWEH-dah deh lah fohr-TOO-nah

7) **carrusel/tiovivo** (carousel/merry-go-round)
kah-rroo-SEHL/tyoh-VEE-voh

8) **carros chocones/autos chocadores** (bumper cars)
KAH-rrohs choh-KOH-nehs/OW-tohs choh-kah-DOH-rehs

9) **tazas giratorias/tazas locas** (teacups/cup and saucer)
TAH-sahs hee-rah-TOH-ryahs/TAH-sahs LOH-kahs

10) **péndulo** (pendulum)
PEHN-doo-loh

11) **sala de juegos** (arcade room)
SAH-lah deh HWEH-gohs

12) **salchicha empanizada/banderilla** (corn dog)
sahl-CHEE-chah ehm-pah-nee-SAH-dah/bahn-deh-REE-yah

13) **granizado** (snow cone)
grah-nee-SAH-doh

14) **algodón de azúcar** (cotton candy)
ahl-goh-DOHN deh ah-SOO-kahr

15) **manzana de caramelo/manzana acaramelada** (candy apple)
mahn-SAH-nah deh kah-rah-MEH-loh/ah-kah-rah-meh-LAH-dah

Su madre no lo dejó subir a la montaña rusa después de que él comiera manzanas acarameladas, salchichas empanizadas y algodón de azúcar.
His mother would not let him ride the roller coaster after he ate candy apples, corn dogs, and cotton candy.

A ella le gusta la emoción de las sillas voladoras, pero a él le gusta la vista desde la rueda de la fortuna.
She likes the excitement of the swing ride, but he likes the view from the Ferris wheel.

EVENTOS EN LA VIDA (LIFE EVENTS)

1) **nacimiento** (birth)
nah-see-MYEHN-toh

2) **bautizo** (christening/baptism)
bow-TEE-soh

3) **comenzar la escuela** (start school)
koh-mehn-SAHR lah ehs-KWEH-lah

4) **hacer amigos** (make friends)
ah-SEHR ah-MEE-gohs

5) **cumpleaños** (birthday)
koom-pleh-AH-nyohs

6) **enamorarse** (fall in love)
eh-nah-moh-RAHR-seh

7) **graduación** (graduation)
grah-dwah-SYOHN

8) **comenzar la universidad** (start university/begin college)
koh-mehn-SAHR lah oo-nee-vehr-see-DAHD

9) **conseguir un empleo** (get a job)
kohn-seh-GEER oon ehm-PLEH-oh

10) **convertirse en emprendedor** (become an entrepreneur)
kohn-vehr-TEER-seh ehn ehm-prehn-deh-DOHR

11) **viajar por el mundo** (travel around the world)
vyah-HAHR pohr ehl MOON-doh

12) **casarse** (get married)
kah-SAHR-seh

13) **tener un bebé** (have a baby)
teh-NEHR oon beh-BEH

14) **celebrar fiestas infantiles** (celebrate children's party)
seh-leh-BRAHR FYEHS-tahs een-fahn-TEE-lehs

15) **jubilación/retiro** (retirement)
hoo-bee-lah-SYOHN/reh-TEE-roh

16) **muerte** (death)
MWEHR-teh

Al casarse, mis padres dijeron "Hasta que la muerte nos separe".
When they got married, my parents said, "Till death do us part."

Conseguí un empleo antes de la graduación
I got a job before graduation.

Ellos quieren esperar para tener un bebé después de viajar por el mundo.
They want to wait to have a baby after traveling around the world.

ADJETIVOS I (ADJECTIVES I)

1) **grande** (big)
   GRAHN-deh

2) **pequeño** (small)
   peh-KEH-nyoh

3) **ruidoso** (loud)
   rrwee-DOH-soh

4) **silencioso** (silent)
   see-lehn-SYOH-soh

5) **largo** (long)
   LAHR-goh

6) **corto** (short)
   KOHR-toh

7) **ancho/amplio** (wide)
   AHN-choh/AHM-plyoh

8) **angosto/estrecho** (narrow)
   ahn-GOHS-toh/ehs-TREH-choh

9) **caro/costoso** (expensive)
   KAH-roh/kohs-TOH-soh

10) **barato** (cheap)
    bah-RAH-toh

11) **rápido** (fast)
    RRAH-pee-doh

12) **lento** (slow)
    LEHN-toh

13) **vacío** (empty)
    vah-SEE-oh

14) **lleno** (full)
    YEH-noh

15) **suave** (soft)
    SWAH-veh

16) **duro** (hard)
    DOO-roh

17) **alto** (tall)
    AHL-toh

18) **bajo** (short)
    BAH-hoh

Las calles largas y angostas y el autobús lleno hicieron duro el viaje.
The long, narrow streets and the full bus made the journey hard.

Ella no es muy baja, pero su novio es extremademente alto.
She is not very short, but her boyfriend is extremely tall.

Ésta cobija es suave, pero muy cara.
This blanket is soft, but very expensive.

QUIZ #6

Use arrows to match the corresponding translations:

a. lobster

b. cotton candy

c. triangle

d. soft

e. book

f. sugar

g. get a job

h. dairy products

i. sign language

j. birth

k. cheeseburger

l. square

m. crab

n. milk

o. loud

p. fried chicken

1. conseguir un empleo

2. cuadrado

3. pollo frito

4. lenguaje de señas

5. leche

6. cangrejo

7. hamburguesa con queso

8. algodón de azúcar

9. nacimiento

10. ruidoso

11. azúcar

12. suave

13. langosta

14. productos lácteos

15. libro

16. triángulo

Fill in the blank spaces with the options below (use each word only once):

Paula y Jessica son muy buenas amigas; cuando salen del trabajo van al restaurante de la esquina a almorzar. A Paula le gusta comer _____ o _____, pero Jessica es vegetariana y prefiere _____ o _____. Por error, les trajeron una pizza _____ con _____. Ellas educadamente devolvieron el pedido, sorprendidas de que esta pizza era un _____ perfecto. Ordenaron las _____ antes de que llegara la comida porque tenían sed, mientras conversaban sobre cómo la vida es una _____ y hablaban de que quieren _____ antes de que llegue el momento de su _____. Definitivamente, quieren conocer esos lugares mágicos que solo han visto en _____.

ensalada de col   jubilación

círculo   pollo

viajar por el mundo   películas

cordero   anchoas

bebidas   montaña rusa

grande   sopa de cebolla

ADJETIVOS II (ADJECTIVES II)

1) **nuevo** (new)
NWEH-voh

2) **viejo** (old)
VYEH-hoh

3) **cómodo** (comfortable)
KOH-moh-doh

4) **incómodo** (uncomfortable)
een-KOH-moh-doh

5) **peligroso** (dangerous)
peh-lee-GROH-soh

6) **irritante/fastidioso** (annoying)
ee-rree-TAHN-teh/fahs-tee-DYOH-soh

7) **tembloroso** (shaky)
tehm-bloh-ROH-soh

8) **completo** (complete)
kohm-PLEH-toh

9) **incompleto** (incomplete)
een-kohm-PLEH-toh

10) **roto** (broken)
RROH-toh

11) **hermoso** (gorgeous)
ehr-MOH-soh

12) **virtuoso** (virtuous)
veer-TWOH-soh

13) **similar** (similar)
see-mee-LAHR

14) **diferente** (different)
dee-feh-REHN-teh

15) **abierto** (open)
ah-BYEHR-toh

16) **cerrado** (closed)
seh-RRAH-doh

Estoy tirando esto porque está viejo y roto.
I am throwing this away because it is old and broken.

Todos dicen que él es hermoso, pero ella solo lo encuentra fastidioso.
Everyone says that he is gorgeous, but she just finds him annoying.

Él se siente incómodo cuando ella deja la puerta abierta.
He feels uncomfortable when she leaves the door open.

ADVERBIOS (ADVERBS)

1) **aquí** (here)
ah-KEE

2) **allá** (there)
ah-YAH

3) **cerca** (near)
SEHR-kah

4) **lejos** (far)
LEH-hohs

5) **arriba** (up)
ah-RREE-bah

6) **abajo** (down)
ah-BAH-ho

7) **dentro/adentro** (inside)
DEHN-troh/ah-DEHN-troh

8) **fuera/afuera** (outside)
FWEH-rah/ah-FWEH-rah

9) **delante/adelante** (ahead)
deh-LAHN-teh/ah-deh-LAHN-teh

10) **atrás/detrás** (behind)
ah-TRAHS/deh-TRAHS

11) **no** (no)
noh

12) **sí** (yes)
see

13) **ahora/ya** (now)
ah-OH-rah/yah

14) **bien** (well/good/right)
byehn

15) **mal** (bad/wrong)
mahl

Cerca o lejos, siempre te llevaré dentro.
Near or far, I will always carry you inside.

Estuve mal anoche, pero me siento bien ahora.
I was doing badly last night, but I feel well now.

Sí, sé quien es, pero no, no la conozco bien.
Yes, I know who she is, but no, I do not know her well.

DIRECCIONES (DIRECTIONS)

1) **manzana/cuadra** (block)
mahn-SAH-nah/KWAH-drah

2) **plaza** (square)
PLAH-sah

3) **parque** (park)
PAHR-keh

4) **metro/subterráneo** (subway)
MEH-troh/soob-teh-RRAH-neh-oh

5) **esquina** (corner)
ehs-KEE-nah

6) **avenida** (avenue)
ah-veh-NEE-dah

7) **calle** (street)
KAH-yeh

8) **parada de autobuses** (bus stop)
pah-RAH-dah deh ow-toh-BOO-sehs

9) **semáforo** (traffic lights)
seh-MAH-foh-roh

10) **cruce/paso peatonal**
(crossing/crosswalk)
KROO-seh/PAH-soh peh-ah-toh-NAHL

11) **arriba** (up)
ah-RREE-bah

12) **abajo** (down)
ah-BAH-hoh

13) **izquierda** (left)
ees-KYEHR-dah

14) **derecha** (right)
deh-REH-chah

15) **señalización vial** (road signs)
seh-nyah-lee-sah-SYOHN vee-AHL

16) **policía de tránsito** (traffic police)
poh-lee-SEE-ah deh TRAHN-see-toh

No hay paradas de autobús en mi calle.
There are no bus stops on my street.

No puedes girar a la derecha en semáforo rojo en esta esquina.
You cannot turn right on a red traffic light at this corner.

El metro te llevará al parque desde la plaza.
The metro will take you to the park from the square.

EL RESTAURANTE (THE RESTAURANT)

1) **gerente** (manager)
heh-REHN-teh

2) **mesa** (table)
MEH-sah

3) **menú** (menu)
meh-NOO

4) **platillo** (dish)
plah-TEE-yoh

5) **aperitivo/entremés** (appetizer)
ah-peh-ree-TEE-voh/ehn-treh-MEHS

6) **entrada** (starter)
ehn-TRAH-dah

7) **plato principal** (main course)
PLAH-toh preen-see-PAHL

8) **postre** (dessert)
POHS-treh

9) **comensal** (diner)
koh-mehn-SAHL

10) **cocinero** (cook)
koh-see-NEH-roh

11) **mesero** (waiter)
meh-SEH-roh

12) **mesera** (waitress)
meh-SEH-rah

13) **propina** (tip)
proh-PEE-nah

14) **silla alta/silla para bebés** (high chair)
SEE-yah AHL-tah/SEE-yah PAH-rah
beh-BEHS

15) **carta de vinos** (wine list)
KAHR-tah deh VEE-nohs

16) **chef pastelero** (pastry chef)
chef pahs-teh-LEH-roh

Éste es mi restaurante favorito para postres y aperitivos.
This is my favorite restaurant for desserts and appetizers.

La mesera hizo un excelente trabajo, así que le dejé una propina generosa.
The waitress did an excellent job, so I left her a generous tip.

No tomamos; no es necesaria la carta de vinos.
We do not drink; the wine list is not necessary.

EL CENTRO COMERCIAL (THE MALL)

1) **piso/planta/nivel** (floor)
PEE-soh/PLAHN-tah/nee-VEHL

2) **acuario** (aquarium)
ah-KWAH-ryoh

3) **patio de comidas/área de comida** (food court)
PAH-tyoh deh koh-MEE-dahs/AH-reh-ah deh koh-MEE-dah

4) **elevador** (elevator)
eh-leh-vah-DOHR

5) **escaleras mecánicas** (escalators)
ehs-kah-LEH-rahs meh-KAH-nee-kahs

6) **salida de emergencia** (emergency exit)
sah-LEE-dah deh eh-mehr-HEN-syah

7) **salón de belleza** (beauty salon)
sah-LOHN deh beh-YEH-sah

8) **tienda de ropa** (clothing store)
TYEHN-dah deh RROH-pah

9) **parque infantil** (playground)
PAHR-keh een-fahn-TEEL

10) **guardia de seguridad** (security guard)
GWAHR-dyah deh see-goo-ree-DAHD

11) **cámara de vigilancia** (surveillance camera)
KAH-mah-rah deh vee-hee-LAHN-syah

12) **panadería** (bakery)
pah-nah-deh-REE-ah

13) **tienda de deportes** (sports store)
TYEHN-dah deh deh-POHR-tehs

14) **fuente** (fountain)
FWEHN-teh

El guardia de seguridad me dijo que tomara el elevador o las escaleras mecánicas al primer piso para llegar al patio de comidas.
The security guard told me to take the elevator or the escalators to the first floor to get to the food court.

La cámara de vigilancia enfrente de la tienda de deportes capturó al ladrón saliendo de la tienda de ropa.
The surveillance camera in front of the sports store captured the thief leaving the clothing store.

Cuando mi esposa va al salón de belleza, compro algo en la panadería y me lo como junto a la fuente.
When my wife goes to the beauty salon, I buy something at the bakery and eat it next to the fountain.

VERBOS I (VERBS I)

1) **hablar** (to talk)
ah-BLAHR

2) **beber** (to drink)
beh-BEHR

3) **comer** (to eat)
koh-MEHR

4) **caminar** (to walk)
kah-mee-NAHR

5) **abrir** (to open)
ah-BREER

6) **cerrar** (to close)
seh-RRAHR

7) **dar** (to give)
dahr

8) **mirar** (to see)
mee-RAHR

9) **seguir** (to follow)
seh-GEER

10) **abrazar** (to hug)
ah-brah-SAHR

11) **besar** (to kiss)
beh-SAHR

12) **comprar** (to buy)
kohm-PRAHR

13) **escuchar** (to listen)
ehs-koo-CHAHR

14) **cantar** (to sing)
kahn-TAHR

15) **bailar** (to dance)
bayh-LAHR

Después de tomar, le gusta cantar, bailar y abrazar a todo el mundo.
After drinking, he likes to sing, dance, and hug everyone.

Solo tuve que mirarla una vez para querer besarla.
I only had to see her once to want to kiss her.

Le voy a comprar el CD, ¡pero espero nunca tener que escucharlo!
I am going to buy her the CD, but I hope I never have to listen to it!

VERBOS II (VERBS II)

1) **escribir** (to write)
ehs-kree-BEER

2) **leer** (to read)
leh-EHR

3) **limpiar** (to clean)
leem-PYAHR

4) **recoger** (to pick up)
rreh-koh-HEHR

5) **encontrar** (to find)
ehn-kohn-TRAHR

6) **lavar** (to wash)
lah-VAHR

7) **observar** (to watch)
ohb-sehr-VAHR

8) **reparar** (to fix)
rreh-pah-RAHR

9) **pensar** (to think)
pehn-SAHR

10) **tomar** (to take)
toh-MAHR

11) **cortar** (to cut)
kohr-TAHR

12) **detener** (to stop)
deh-teh-NEHR

13) **llorar** (to cry)
yoh-RAHR

14) **sonreír** (to smile)
sohn-rreh-EER

15) **ayudar** (to help)
ah-yoo-DAHR

Si quieres escribir, debes leer.
If you want to write, you must read.

Empezó a llorar y no lo pude detener.
He started crying and I could not stop him.

La iba a recoger, pero no la pude encontrar.
I was going to pick her up, but I could not find her.

152

CONSTRUCCIÓN I (CONSTRUCTION I)

1) **grúa** (crane)
GROO-ah

2) **cinta de seguridad** (hazard tape)
SEEN-tah deh seh-goo-ree-DAHD

3) **cono de tráfico/cono de señalización**
(traffic cone)
KOH-noh deh TRAH-fee-koh/seh-nyah-lee-sah-SYOHN

4) **pala de construcción** (construction shovel)
PAH-lah deh kohns-trook-SYOHN

5) **martillo** (hammer)
mahr-TEE-yoh

6) **cortaalambres/cortador de cables**
(wire cutters)
kohr-tah-ah-LAHM-brehs/kohr-tah-DOHR deh KAH-blehs

7) **rodillo de pintura** (paint roller)
rroh-DEE-yoh deh peen-TOO-rah

8) **motosierra** (chainsaw)
moh-toh-SYEH-rrah

9) **taladro/perforadora** (drill)
tah-LAH-droh/pehr-foh-rah-DOH-rah

10) **martillo neumático** (jackhammer)
mahr-TEE-yoh neh-oo-MAH-tee-koh

11) **alicates/tenazas** (pliers)
ah-lee-KAH-tehs/teh-NAH-sahs

12) **destornillador** (screwdriver)
dehs-tohr-nee-yah-DOHR

No pude llegar a mi casa porque había conos de tráfico y cinta de seguridad rodeando mi vecindario.
I could not get home because there were traffic cones and hazard tape surrounding my neighborhood.

Eso es un cortaalambres; pedí alicates.
That is a wire cutter; I asked for pliers.

Como no tenía taladro, hizo el agujero con un martillo y un destornillador.
Since he did not have a drill, he made the hole with a hammer and a screwdriver.

CONSTRUCCIÓN II (CONSTRUCTION II)

1) **caja de herramientas** (toolbox)
KAH-hah deh eh-rrah-MYEHN-tahs

2) **casco de seguridad** (work helmet/hard hat)
KAHS-koh deh seh-goo-ree-DAHD

3) **plano/modelo** (blueprint)
PLAH-noh/moh-DEH-loh

4) **tuberías/tubos** (pipes)
too-beh-REE-ahs/TOO-bohs

5) **paleta/espátula** (trowel)
pah-LEH-tah/ehs-PAH-too-lah

6) **mezcladora de concreto/hormigonera** (concrete mixer)
mehs-klah-DOH-rah deh kohn-KREH-toh/ohr-mee-gohn-NEH-rah

7) **ladrillo** (brick)
lah-DREE-yoh

8) **materiales de construcción** (building materials)
mah-teh-RYAH-lehs deh kohns-trook-SYOHN

9) **baldosas/losas** (tiles)
bahl-DOH-sahs/LOH-sahs

10) **cemento** (cement)
seh-MEHN-toh

11) **arena** (sand)
ah-REH-nah

12) **grava** (gravel)
GRAH-vah

En la mezcladora de concreto mezcla una parte de cemento con tres partes de arena y seis partes de grava.
In the concrete mixer, mix one part cement with three parts sand and six parts gravel.

Es rápido con una paleta y un ladrillo.
He is quick with a trowel and a brick.

El plomero no revisará las tuberías hasta que le demos los planos.
The plumber will not check the pipes until we give him the blueprints.

QUIZ #7

Use arrows to match the corresponding translations:

a. building materials

b. to clean

c. surveillance camera

d. down

e. crane

f. to sing

g. cook

h. here

i. dangerous

j. cement

k. to find

l. sports store

m. street

n. manager

o. ahead

p. to hug

1. cemento

2. gerente

3. calle

4. encontrar

5. abrazar

6. materiales de construcción

7. tienda de deportes

8. delante / adelante

9. cocinero

10. limpiar

11. abajo

12. cantar

13. cámara de vigilancia

14. peligroso

15. aquí

16. grúa

Fill in the blank spaces with the options below (use each word only once):

Víctor es un chico _____ a los demás de su escuela, se siente _____ cuando hay mucho ruido a su alrededor y no le gusta _____ con nadie. Como le disgustan las multitudes, prefiere _____ hacia su casa en lugar de _____ el autobús o el metro. Una tarde iba por la _____ y pasó _____ de un centro comercial donde están construyendo un _____, llevándose un gran susto cuando encendieron una _____ y tropezando con una _____ que estaba en la acera. Su primera reacción fue molestarse, pues quedó con la cara llena de _____, pero terminó riéndose y comprando un _____ para pasar el susto.

motosierra	hablar
caminar	avenida
acuario	cerca
arena	incómodo
diferente	caja de herramientas
postre	tomar

PLANTAS Y ÁRBOLES (PLANTS AND TREES)

1) **flor silvestre** (wildflower)
flohr seel-VEHS-treh

2) **hierba** (herb)
YEHR-bah

3) **seta** (mushroom)
SEH-tah

4) **maleza** (weed)
mah-LEH-sah

5) **alga** (seaweed)
AHL-gah

6) **helecho** (fern)
eh-LEH-choh

7) **caña/junco** (reed)
KAH-nyah/HOON-koh

8) **bambú** (bamboo)
bahm-BOO

9) **hiedra** (ivy)
YEH-drah

10) **musgo** (moss)
MOOS-goh

11) **césped** (grass)
SEHS-pehd

12) **palmera/palma** (palm tree)
pahl-MEH-rah/PAHL-mah

13) **manglar** (mangrove)
mahn-GLAHR

14) **cactus** (cactus)
KAHK-toos

El suelo es horrible aquí, así que las únicas plantas que crecen bien son las flores silvestres y la maleza.
The soil is terrible here, so the only plants that grow well are wildflowers and weeds.

Mi mama tenía helechos, hierbas y palmas en su jardín, pero yo apenas puedo cuidar un cactus.
My mother had ferns, herbs, and palm trees in her garden, but I can barely take care of a cactus.

El musgo y las algas son dos posibles fuentes alimenticias futuras.
Moss and seaweed are two possible future food sources.

EL CARNAVAL (THE CARNIVAL)

1) **máscara/antifaz** (mask)
   MAHS-kah-rah/ahn-tee-FAHS

2) **disfraz** (costume/disguise)
   dees-FRAHS

3) **carroza** (float)
   kah-RROH-sah

4) **flores** (flowers)
   FLOH-rehs

5) **redoblante** (snare drum)
   rreh-doh-BLAHN-teh

6) **payaso** (clown)
   pah-YAH-soh

7) **superhéroe** (superhero)
   soo-pehr-EH-roh-eh

8) **princesa** (princess)
   preen-SEH-sah

9) **astronauta** (astronaut)
   ahs-troh-NOW-tah

10) **mimo** (mime)
    MEE-moh

11) **prisionero** (prisoner)
    pree-syoh-NEH-roh

12) **electrodoméstico** (household appliance)
    eh-lehk-troh-doh-MEHS-tee-koh

13) **hada** (fairy)
    AH-dah

14) **leñador** (lumberjack)
    leh-nyah-DOHR

Mi hija era una princesa en la carroza con las flores.
My daughter was a princess on the float with the flowers.

Mi hijo quería ser un payaso o un mimo, pero lo convencí de ser un superhéroe.
My son wanted to be a clown or a mime, but I convinced him to be a superhero.

No había disfraces de astronauta, así que fui de leñador.
There were no astronaut costumes, so I went as a lumberjack.

EL TALLER (THE WORKSHOP)

1) **herramienta** (tool)
eh-rrah-MYEHN-tah

2) **talabartería** (saddlery)
tah-lah-bahr-teh-REE-ah

3) **carpintería** (carpentry/woodwork)
kahr-peen-teh-REE-ah

4) **tapicería** (upholstery/tapestry)
tah-pee-seh-REE-ah

5) **zapatería** (shoemaking/shoerepair)
sah-pah-teh-REE-ah

6) **orfebrería** (silversmith)
ohr-feh-breh-REE-ah

7) **herrería** (blacksmith)
eh-rreh-REE-ah

8) **mecánica** (mechanic)
meh-KAH-nee-kah

9) **textil** (textile)
tehks-TEEL

10) **panadería** (bakery)
pah-nah-deh-REE-ah

11) **bisutería** (costume jewelry)
bee-soo-teh-REE-ah

12) **calzado** (footwear)
kahl-SAH-doh

13) **mantenimiento** (maintenance)
mahn-teh-nee-MYEHN-toh

14) **reparación** (repair)
rreh-pah-rah-SYOHN

15) **pintura** (painting)
peen-TOO-rah

16) **repostería** (pastry)
rreh-pohs-teh-REE-ah

Su padre quiso que su hijo lo siguiera en su negocio de carpintería, pero el joven quería dedicar su vida a la pintura.
His father wanted his son to follow him in his carpentry business, but the young man wanted to dedicate his life to painting.

Puedo hacer las reparaciones, pero no soy el personal de mantenimiento.
I can do the repairs, but I am not the maintenance personel.

Él tiene todas las herramientas para la zapatería, pero eso no lo convierte en zapatero.
He has all the tools for shoerepairing, but that does not make him a shoemaker.

LA TIENDA DE COMESTIBLES (THE GROCERY STORE)

1) **pasta** (pasta)
PAHS-tah

2) **arroz** (rice)
ah-RROHS

3) **avena** (oat)
ah-VEH-nah

4) **pan** (bread)
pahn

5) **aceites** (oils)
ah-SEYH-tehs

6) **salsas** (sauces)
SAHL-sahs

7) **aderezos para ensaladas** (salad dressings)
ah-deh-REH-sohs PAH-rah ehn-sah-LAH-das

8) **condimentos** (condiments)
kohn-dee-MEHN-tos

9) **enlatados** (canned goods)
ehn-lah-TAH-dohs

10) **jamón** (ham)
hah-MOHN

11) **queso** (cheese)
KEH-soh

12) **mantequilla de maní** (peanut butter)
mahn-teh-KEE-yah deh mah-NEE

13) **dulces/caramelos** (candy)
DOOL-sehs/kah-rah-MEH-los

14) **frijoles** (beans)
free-HOH-lehs

15) **café** (coffee)
kah-FEH

16) **té** (tea)
teh

Prefiero un desayuno sencillo de pan con mantequilla de maní y una taza de café.
I prefer a simple breakfast of bread with peanut butter and a cup of coffee.

A él le encantan las salsas, los condimentos y los aderezos para ensaladas, pero todos le dan dolor de estómago.
He loves sauces, condiments, and salad dressings, but they all give him a stomachache.

Ella sirve pasta o arroz con cada comida.
She serves pasta or rice with every meal.

VIAJE Y HOSPEDAJE I (TRAVEL AND LIVING I)

1) **anfitrión** (host)
ahn-fee-TRYOHN

2) **turista** (tourist)
too-REES-tah

3) **viajero** (traveler)
vyah-HEH-roh

4) **equipaje** (luggage)
eh-kee-PAH-heh

5) **equipaje de mano** (hand luggage)
eh-kee-PAH-heh deh MAH-noh

6) **cámara** (camera)
KAH-mah-rah

7) **hotel** (hotel)
oh-TEHL

8) **hostal** (hostel)
ohs-TAHL

9) **pensión/posada** (Bed & Breakfast/inn)
pehn-SYOHN/poh-SAH-dah

10) **cabaña** (cabin)
kah-BAH-nyah

11) **carpa** (tent)
KAHR-pah

12) **vuelo** (flight)
voo-EH-loh

13) **salida** (departure)
sah-LEE-dah

14) **llegada** (arrival)
yeh-GAH-dah

Las posadas y hosteles son demasiado sociales para mí; prefiero hospedarme en un hotel cuando ando de turista.
Inns and hostels are too social for me; I prefer to stay in hotels when I'm a tourist.

Su esposo solía dormir en una carpa cuando iban al bosque, pero ella inisiste en que renten una cabaña.
Her husband used to sleep in a tent when they went to the woods, but she insists they rent a cabin.

Ellos intentan ser discretos con sus cámaras para no parecer turistas.
They try to be discrete with their cameras so that they don't look like tourists.

VIAJE Y HOSPEDAJE II (TRAVEL AND LIVING II)

1) **pueblo** (town)
PWEH-bloh

2) **mapa** (map)
MAH-pah

3) **parada de autobuses** (bus stop)
pah-RAH-dah deh ow-toh-BOO-sehs

4) **taxi** (taxi)
TAHK-see

5) **alquiler de autos** (car rental)
ahl-kee-LEHR deh OW-tohs

6) **estación de trenes** (train station)
ehs-tah-SYOHN deh TREH-nehs

7) **aeropuerto** (airport)
ah-eh-roh-PWER-toh

8) **pasaporte** (passport)
pah-sah-POHR-teh

9) **documento de identidad/tarjeta de identificación** (ID/identification card)
doh-koo-MEHN-toh deh ee-dehn-tee-DAHD/tahr-HEH-tah deh ee-dehn-tee-fee-kah-SYOHN

10) **moneda** (currency)
moh-NEH-dah

11) **efectivo** (cash)
eh-fek-TEE-voh

12) **tarjeta de débito** (debit card)
tahr-HEH-tah deh DEH-bee-toh

13) **tarjeta de crédito** (credit card)
tahr-HEH-tah deh KREH-dee-toh

14) **guía turístico** (tourist guide)
GEE-ah too-REES-tee-koh

Uso tarjeta de débito para la mayoría de mis compras, así que rara vez tengo efectivo.
I use a debit card for most of my purchases, so I rarely have cash.

Con el GPS, no necesitamos mapa, pero sería de ayuda un guía turístico.
With the GPS, we do not need a map, but a tourist guide would be helpful.

Perdí mi vuelo porque el taxi me llevó a la estación de trenes en vez de al aeropuerto.
I missed my flight because the taxi took me to the train station instead of the airport.

JUGUETES (TOYS)

1) **pelota/balón** (ball)
peh-LOH-tah/bah-LOHN

2) **oso de peluche** (teddy bear)
OH-soh deh peh-LOO-cheh

3) **tren** (train)
trehn

4) **patineta** (skateboard)
pah-tee-NEH-tah

5) **muñeca** (doll)
moo-NYEH-kah

6) **auto de carreras** (race car)
OW-toh deh kah-RREH-rahs

7) **robot** (robot)
rroh-BOHT

8) **cometa** (kite)
koh-MEH-tah

9) **tambor** (drum)
tahm-BOHR

10) **hula hula** (hula hoop)
OO-lah OO-lah

11) **vagón** (wagon)
vah-GOHN

12) **cubos** (blocks)
KOO-bohs

13) **xilófono** (xylophone)
ksee-LOH-foh-noh

14) **camión** (truck)
kah-MYOHN

15) **avión** (airplane)
ah-VYOHN

16) **bloques** (bricks)
BLOH-kehs

Al niño de al lado le gusta jugar con trenes y camiones, pero su hermano juega con muñecas.
The boy next door likes playing with trains and trucks, but his brother plays with dolls.

Tengo cubos y bloques para los niños del vecindario.
I have blocks and bricks for the neighborhood kids.

Fernando está aprendiendo a montar en patineta, pero Byron prefiere su bicicleta.
Fernando is learning to ride a skateboard, but Byron prefers his bicycle.

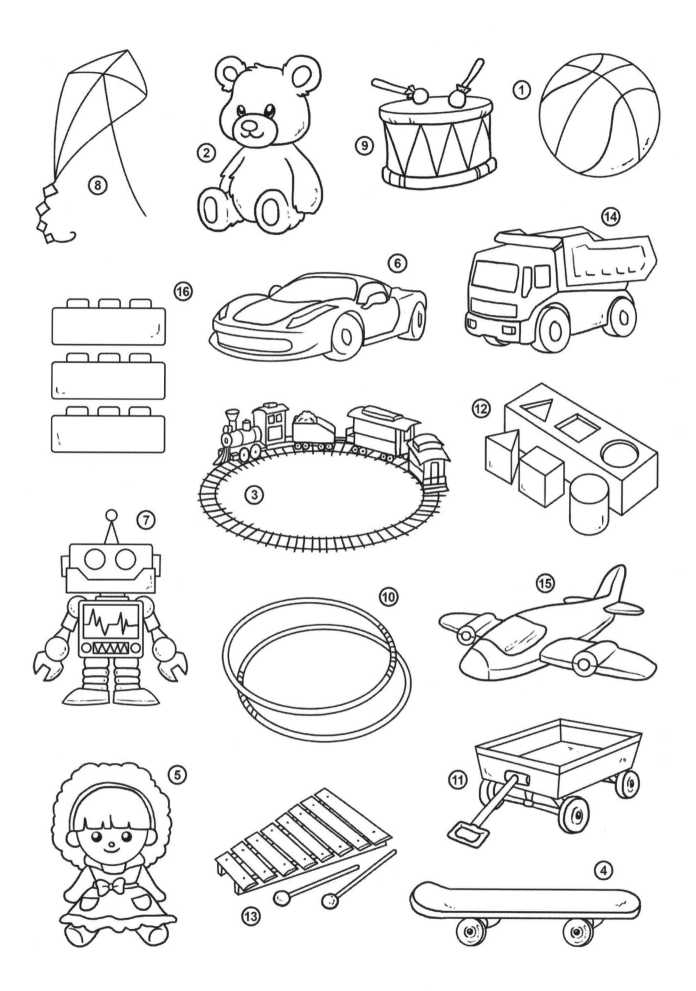

LA FIESTA DE CUMPLEAÑOS (THE BIRTHDAY PARTY)

1) **pancarta/cartel de cumpleaños**
   (birthday banner)
   pahn-KAHR-tah/kahr-TEHL deh
   koom-pleh-AH-nyohs

2) **decoración** (decoration)
   deh-koh-rah-SYOHN

3) **presente/regalo** (present/gift)
   preh-SEHN-teh/rreh-GAH-loh

4) **mantel** (tableware)
   mahn-TEHL

5) **cumpleañero** (birthday person)
   koom-pleh-ah-NYEH-roh

6) **globo** (balloon)
   GLOH-boh

7) **pastel de cumpleaños** (birthday cake)
   pahs-TEHL deh koom-pleh-AH-nyohs

8) **platos** (plates)
   PLAH-tohs

9) **tenedores** (forks)
   teh-neh-DOH-rehs

10) **cucharas** (spoons)
    koo-CHAH-rahs

11) **vasos** (cups)
    VAH-sohs

12) **pajilla/pitillo/popote** (straw)
    pah-HEE-yah/pee-TEE-yoh/poh-POH-teh

13) **piñata** (piñata)
    pee-NYAH-tah

14) **vela** (candle)
    VEH-lah

15) **sombrero** (hat)
    sohm-BREH-roh

16) **invitados** (guests)
    een-vee-TAH-dohs

A mí no me importa tanto el regalo mientras me den mi pastel de cumpleaños.
I do not care much about the present as long as I get my birthday cake.

Ya tenemos vasos y platos. ¿Puedes traer tenedores y cucharas?
We already have glasses and plates. Can you bring forks and spoons?

El cumpleañero quiso globos y una piñata.
The birthday boy wanted balloons and a piñata.

OPUESTOS (OPPOSITES)

1) **limpio** (clean)
LEEM-pyoh

2) **sucio** (dirty)
SOO-syoh

3) **pocos** (few)
POH-kohs

4) **muchos** (many)
MOO-chohs

5) **ataque** (attack)
ah-TAH-keh

6) **defensa** (defense)
deh-FEHN-sah

7) **recto** (straight)
RREHK-toh

8) **curvo** (curved)
KOOR-voh

9) **juntos** (together)
HOON-tohs

10) **separados** (separated)
seh-pah-RAH-dohs

11) **joven** (young)
HOH-vehn

12) **viejo** (old)
VYEH-hoh

13) **abundancia** (wealth)
ah-boon-DAHN-syah

14) **carencia** (shortage)
kah-REHN-syah

15) **cóncavo** (concave)
KOHN-kah-voh

16) **convexo** (convex)
kohn-VEHK-soh

El joven y el viejo están separados.
The young man and the old man are separated.

Muchos son llamados, pero pocos son elegidos.
Many are called, but few are chosen.

Las artes marciales son para la defensa, no para el ataque.
Martial arts are for defense, not attack.

QUIZ #8

Use arrows to match the corresponding translations:

a. rice

b. candle

c. host

d. tent

e. silversmith

f. mangrove

g. kite

h. mask

i. straight

j. race car

k. peanut butter

l. seaweed

m. together

n. balloon

o. town

p. footwear

1. mantequilla de maní

2. alga

3. globo

4. calzado

5. recto

6. arroz

7. juntos

8. auto de carreras

9. pueblo

10. vela

11. manglar

12. orfebrería

13. anfitrión

14. máscara / antifaz

15. carpa

16. cometa

Fill in the blank spaces with the options below (use each word only once):

Llegó el día tan ansiado para Katherine y Samuel, y tenían planeado hasta el más mínimo detalle. La boda tenía que ser perfecta. Tenían todo preparado: la _____, los _____, la música, la mesa de _____... La familia del novio tenía una _____, por lo que se ofrecieron a encargarse de la _____; no querían dejar algo tan importante en manos de cualquier persona. El salón estaba listo para el evento, con adornos de _____ y una que otra _____. La novia se sentía como una _____ en su vestido blanco, más hermoso de lo que había soñado. Luego, irían a la _____ que habían rentado en las montañas para su luna de miel, y ya tenían un _____ marcado con la ruta que seguirían y los lugares que visitarían. Aunque ya tenían los boletos de _____, estaban nerviosos de que algo saliera mal... pero decidieron concentrarse en lo bien que la estaban pasando, sabiendo que aún les quedaban _____ días, meses y años felices por delante, como para preocuparse en ese momento.

panadería	decoración
flor silvestre	mapa
muchos	princesa
avión	repostería
cabaña	bambú
quesos	invitados

CONCLUSION

While there is certainly much more to say about the Spanish language, we hope this general overview helps you in understanding and using the words and phrases in this dictionary, as well as your own words and phrases as you continue on your journey to bilingualism.

We would like to leave you with a few suggestions for a pleasant and fruitful language learning experience:

1. Learn what you need and what you love.

   While survival Spanish is indispensable, mechanical memorization of long lists of words is not the best use of your time and energy. Make sure to focus on the vocabulary that is important and useful to you in your life. If you are a sportsperson or an artist or an interior decorator, seek words in that area (and if you are not, do not!).

2. Find bridges to understanding in simple sentence patterns that you can apply to multiple situations. For example:

   a. When practicing *ser/estar*, describe everyone you can think of. The short, declarative sentences are perfect for adding adjectives and practicing the verbs. *Ella es delgada, inteligente y seria.* (She is thin, smart, and serious.)

   b. To study verbs, use *(No) Me gusta + verbo* (I (do not) like). *Me gusta cocinar / no me gusta correr, etc.* (I like to cook / I do not like to run, etc.)

3. Use available media to practice all aspects of the language. Movies, music, social media, etc. provide the opportunity to practice reading, writing, and listening at any time from your phone or computer.

4. Practice speaking as soon as you can with a native speaker.

   They will not laugh at you, although they might laugh with you! Spanish speakers are, on the whole, delighted to know that someone is trying to learn their language and will gladly help you. *Warning: This may lead to lifelong friendships and endless invitations to scrumptious feasts.*

5. Remember: **Communication before perfection**. It takes years to master an instrument, but you can play Hot Cross Buns on the first day, and that is progress. You are speaking Spanish from the first *Hola*, and you will be more bilingual every day if you keep practicing.

6. Enjoy the journey!

ANSWERS

QUIZ #1

a-8. b-5. c-11. d-15. e-1. f-14. g-16. h-7. i-13. j-2. k-10. l-9. m-3. n-12. o-6. p-4.

Andrea estaba alimentando a su **gato**, Kif, el sábado en la mañana, antes de ir a casa de su **abuela**. Él no quería comer y se veía **enfermo**, tenía los ojos **tristes**, así que lo llevó al veterinario. Allí le revisaron el **estómago** y vieron que se había tragado ¡un **canario** de juguete! Tuvieron que hacerle una cirugía de emergencia, pero todo salió bien, Kif es tan fuerte como un **león**. Andrea se sintió muy **feliz**, aunque no pudo ir a ver a sus **abuelos**. Lo único bueno fue que evitó que le preguntaran otra vez por qué sigue **soltera**; ella no se siente lista para ese **compromiso**, pues sabe que es una gran **responsabilidad**.

QUIZ # 2

a-10. b-14. c-5. d-13. e-11. f-16. g-12. h-3. i-1. j-15. k-9. l-2. m-6. n-8. o-4. p-7.

Durante la primavera mi familia y yo solemos ir a **plantar algunas flores** al bosque. Siempre llevamos ropa cómoda, como **pantalones cargo**, y el **repelente de insectos** no puede faltar para alejar a las **moscas** y **mosquitos**. Me encanta **ir a una caminata** con mi hermano, incluso si el clima está **lluvioso**. A veces, me da miedo encontrarme con un **oso**, un **leopardo** o un **cocodrilo**, pero mamá dice que no viven en esa zona. Al volver a casa cenaremos un delicioso **bagre/pez gato**, es la especialidad de papá en la cocina, tomaremos **limonada** y nos reiremos de todo lo que sucedió en el viaje.

QUIZ # 3

a-5.   b-9.   c-12.   d-7.   e-16.   f-15.   g-13.   h-14.   i-2.   j-3.   k-6.   l-1.   m-11.
n-4.   o-8.   p-10.

David tenía una reunión importante al **atardecer**, pero se quedó dormido y se la perdió. Al **día** siguiente invitó a sus socios a una gran **cena de Acción de Gracias** para disculparse por haber faltado. David ordenó la mejor **comida** que pudo encontrar, ellos dejaron sus autos en la **entrada/calzada**, y todos cenaron frente a la **chimenea**. Luego, fue al **refrigerador** y buscó los ingredientes para preparar un **chocolate caliente**, pues comenzaron a tener frío. También buscó unas **mantas de lana/cobijas de lana**. En ese momento, pasó frente al **espejo** y se dio cuenta de que tenía una mancha de salsa en el rostro, así que quiso limpiarse con una **servilleta**, pero no fue suficiente; fue rápidamente al baño y se limpió con **jabón**, volviendo a la reunión como si nada hubiese pasado para seguir disfrutando de la agradable velada.

QUIZ # 4

a-5.   b-10.   c-7.   d-14.   e-3.   f-12.   g-1.   h-9.   i-16.   j-2.   k-6.   l-4.
m-15.   n-11.   o-8.   p-10.

Martha es una **estudiante** universitaria que quiere ser **ingeniera**. En sus ratos libres ama estar al aire libre, ir a la **playa** a practicar **surf** y también practicar **ciclismo**, yendo a todos lados en su **bicicleta**. En diciembre se atravesó un perro en su camino, entonces ella se lanzó hacia un **arbusto** para no lastimarlo y ensució su traje de **elfo de Navidad**. Por suerte, el **detergente de lavandería** fue suficiente para quitar el sucio, y la **secadora** hizo el resto del trabajo. Si su **jefe** lo nota, seguramente no le gustará… aunque no le dirá nada ¡porque él es **Santa Claus/Papá Noel**!

QUIZ # 5

a-6.   b-13.   c-8.   d-12.   e-2.   f-10.   g-16.   h-4.   i-15.   j-3.   k-1.   l-14.   m-9.   n-7.
o-5.   p-11.

Lucas trabaja como **investigador** para un observatorio astronómico en un pueblo al **este** de **Asia**. Cuando era niño vivía en una granja, cuidando el **ganado** y ayudando a sus padres a sembrar **sandía** y **maíz**, entre otras cosas. En las noches le gustaba ver la **luna**, pero también miraba el cielo esperando que pasara una **estrella fugaz** mientras su madre tocaba la **armónica**. Allí se enamoró de la astronomía. Una noche se encontró sin querer con una **colmena**, y las avispas salieron furiosas a atacarlo mientras él corría hacia la casa. Sus padres lo llevaron al hospital de inmediato, pues era alérgico a las picaduras de insectos, y lo atendió una **enfermera** muy amable. Con un **dispositivo** muy curioso le inyectó epinefrina, y todos se sintieron muy aliviados de que solo fue un susto.

QUIZ # 6

a-13.   b-8.   c-16.   d-12.   e-15.   f-11.   g-1.   h-14.   i-4.   j-9.   k-7.   l-2.   m-6.   n-5. o-10.   p-3.

Paula y Jessica son muy buenas amigas; cuando salen del trabajo van al restaurante de la esquina a almorzar. A Paula le gusta comer **pollo** o **cordero**, pero Jessica es vegetariana y prefiere **sopa de cebolla** o **ensalada de col**. Por error, les trajeron una pizza **grande** con **anchoas**. Ellas educadamente devolvieron el pedido, sorprendidas de que esta pizza era un **círculo** perfecto. Ordenaron las **bebidas** antes de que llegara la comida porque tenían sed, mientras conversaban sobre cómo la vida es una **montaña rusa** y hablaban de que quieren **viajar por el mundo** antes de que llegue el momento de su **jubilación**. Definitivamente, quieren conocer esos lugares mágicos que solo han visto en **películas**.

QUIZ # 7

a-6.   b-10.   c-13.   d-11.   e-16.   f-12.   g-9.   h-15.   i-14.   j-1.   k-4.   l-7.   m-3.   n-2. o-8.   p-5.

Víctor es un chico **diferente** a los demás de su escuela, se siente **incómodo** cuando hay mucho ruido a su alrededor y no le gusta **hablar** con nadie. Como le disgustan las multitudes, prefiere **caminar** hacia su casa en lugar de **tomar** el autobús o el metro. Una tarde iba por la **avenida** y pasó **cerca** de un centro comercial donde están construyendo un **acuario**, llevándose un gran susto cuando encendieron una **motosierra** y tropezando con una **caja de herramientas** que estaba en la acera. Su primera reacción fue molestarse, pues quedó con la cara llena de **arena**, pero terminó riéndose y comprando un **postre** para pasar el susto.

QUIZ # 8

a-6.   b-10.   c-13.   d-15.   e-12.   f-11.   g-16.   h-14.   i-5.   j-8.   k-1.   l-2.   m-7.   n-3. o-9.   p-4.

Llegó el día tan ansiado para Katherine y Samuel, y tenían planeado hasta el más mínimo detalle. La boda tenía que ser perfecta. Tenían todo preparado: la **decoración**, los **invitados**, la música, la mesa de **quesos**… La familia del novio tenía una **panadería**, por lo que se ofrecieron a encargarse de la **repostería**; no querían dejar algo tan importante en manos de cualquier persona. El salón estaba listo para el evento, con adornos de **bambú** y una que otra **flor silvestre**. La novia se sentía como una **princesa** en su vestido blanco, más hermoso de lo que había soñado. Luego, irían a la **cabaña** que habían rentado en las montañas para su luna de miel, y ya tenían un **mapa** marcado con la ruta que seguirían y los lugares que visitarían. Aunque ya tenían los boletos de **avión**, estaban nerviosos de que algo saliera mal… pero decidieron concentrarse en lo bien que la estaban pasando, sabiendo que aún les quedaban **muchos** días, meses y años felices por delante, como para preocuparse en ese momento.

MORE BOOKS BY LINGO MASTERY

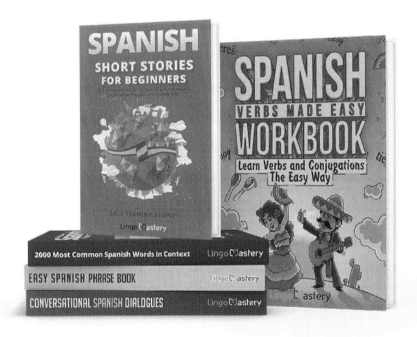

We are not done teaching you Spanish until you're fluent!

Here are some other titles you might find useful in your journey of mastering Spanish:

- **Spanish Short Stories for Beginners**
- **Spanish Verbs Made Easy Workbook**
- **2000 Most Common Spanish Words in Context**
- **Conversational Spanish Dialogues**

But we got many more!

Check out all of our titles at **www.LingoMastery.com/spanish**

Printed in Great Britain
by Amazon

86487330R00111